The Muvipix.com Guide to
CyberLink PowerDirector 19 Ultimate

Steve Grisetti

The fun, easy, powerful way to
make great-looking movies on your
personal computer.

About Muvipix.com

Muvipix.com was created to offer support and community to amateur and semi-professional videomakers. Registration is free, and that gets you access to the world's friendliest, most helpful forum and lots of ad-free space for displaying your work. On the products page, you'll find dozens of free tips, tutorials, motion backgrounds, DVD templates, sound effects, royalty-free music and stock video clips. For a small annual subscription fee that we use to keep the site running, you'll have unlimited downloads from the ever-growing library of support materials and media.

We invite you to drop by and visit our thriving community. It costs absolutely nothing – and we'd love to have you join the neighborhood!

http://Muvipix.com

About the author

Steve Grisetti holds a master's degree in Telecommunications from Ohio University and spent several years working in the motion picture and television industry in Los Angeles. A veteran user of several video editing programs and systems, Steve is the co-founder of Muvipix.com, a help and support site for amateur and semi-professional videomakers. A professional graphic designer and video freelancer, he has taught classes in Photoshop, lectured on design and created classes for lynda.com. He lives in suburban Milwaukee.

Other books by Steve Grisetti

The Muvipix.com Guides to Adobe Premiere Elements 7, 8, 9, 10, 11, 12, 13, 14, 15, 2018, 2019, 2020 and 2021
The Muvipix.com Guides to Photoshop Elements & Premiere Elements 7, 8, 9, 10, 11, 12, 13, 14, 15 and Photoshop Elements 2018, 2019, 2020 and 2021
Cool Tricks & Hot Tips for Adobe Premiere Elements
The Muvipix.com Guide to Adobe Premiere Rush
The Muvipix.com Guide to DVD Architect
The Muvipix.com Guides to Vegas Movie Studio HD 10 and 11
The Muvipix.com Guides to Sony Movie Studio 12 and 13
The Muvipix.com Guide to Vegas Movie Studio Platinum 14, 15, 16 and 17
The Muvipix.com Guides to CyberLink PowerDirector 12, 13, 14, 15, 16, 17 and 18

An Introduction

Once again the folks at CyberLink have figured out a way to pack the most feature-packed consumer editing program in the world with even more features.

The program already included a multi-camera editor, 3D and 360 editing workspaces and the ability to use project files as media in other projects – features usually only found in professional video editing programs. But version 19 now includes tools for designing and animating custom masks, advanced color matching and tools for creating custom title and graphic overlay animations.

CyberLink has also tweaked the interface, reducing clutter while making some of its more advanced tools even easier to access.

In short, once again the folks at CyberLink have figured out how to make this already great editor a little bit better. And, considering how many cool features the program already had, that's no mean feat.

Our goal with our book, as always, is to introduce you to each of these old and new features.. To take you step-by-step through all of its processes. And, along the way, to offer you some tips and tricks for helping make your video editing work flow a little more smoothly.

We also hope you'll check out our web site, Muvipix.com, where we offer free basic training, an ever-growing library of tutorials and lots of royalty-free music, video backgrounds and graphics.

And it's a great place to make new friends and ask questions.

Muvipix.com was created in 2006 as a community and a learning center for videomakers at a variety of levels. Our community includes everyone from amateurs and hobbyists to semi-pros, professionals and even people with broadcast experience. You won't find more knowledgeable, helpful people anywhere else on the Web. I very much encourage you to drop by our forums and say hello. At the very least, you'll make some new friends. And it's rare that there's a question posted there that isn't quickly and enthusiastically answered.

Our learning center consists of video tutorials, tips and, of course, books. But we also offer a wealth of support in the form of custom-created DVD and BluRay disc menus, motion background videos, licensed music and even stock footage. Much of it is absolutely free – and there's even more available for those who purchase one of our affordable site subscriptions.

Our goal has always been to help people get up to speed making great videos and, once they're there, provide them with the inspiration and means to get better and better at doing so.

Why? Because we know making movies and taking great pictures is a heck of a lot of fun – and we want to share that fun with everyone!

Our books, then, are a manifestation of that goal. And my hope for you is that this book helps *you* get up to speed. I think you'll find that, once you learn the basics, making movies on your home computer is a lot more fun than you ever imagined! And you may even amaze yourself with the results in the process.

Thanks for supporting Muvipix.com, and happy moviemaking!

Steve
http://Muvipix.com

The Muvipix.com Guide to CyberLink PowerDirector 19 Ultimate

Section 1: PowerDirector Basics

Table of Contents

Chapter 7

Edit MultiCam Video 87

Cutting between camera angles

Table of Contents

Table of Contents

Section 4: Output Your Finished Movie

Section 1

PowerDirector Basics

Get to Know the PowerDirector Workspaces

Basic Video Editing Moves

What's New in Version 19?

Chapter 1

Get to Know PowerDirector 19

What's what and what it does

There's a lot to love about CyberLink PowerDirector.

It's a remarkably accessible program, even if you've never edited video on your computer before. But it's also surprisingly deep, with features usually reserved for professional editing software.

Rooms   Libraries   Workspaces   Preview Window

The Timeline

Welcome to easy yet powerful moviemaking!

CyberLink's PowerDirector is one of the most user-friendly video editors on the market. Even if you've never edited video before, you should find yourself very quickly finding your way around.

Yet it's also surprisingly deep, including a few features usually only found in professional editing software. The Multicam Designer itself puts this program a cut above the competition.

PowerDirector is designed to keep your workspace as uncluttered and as easy to navigate as possible. Major workspaces and "**Designer**" panels are launched by clicking buttons and tabs, and libraries of media and effects are accessed through various "rooms".

In this chapter, we'll explore these various rooms as well as look at the program's interface (and how to customize it). Then we'll walk you through the basics of video editing in PowerDirector. It's sort of the broad strokes before we go into the details in subsequent chapters.

In subsequent chapters we'll also look at PowerDirector's semi-automatic **Auto Mode** and **Slideshow Creator**, simple workspaces for creating great-looking videos and slideshows from your still photos and images.

PowerDirector Rooms

The various "**Rooms**" in PowerDirector are accessed by clicking the icons or tabs that run along the upper left side of the interface. Each of these **Rooms** includes a library or a set of tools for working on a particular aspect of your movie.

The Media Room

The **Media Room** is where you gather the video, audio, still photos, graphics and music that you will use to create your movie. Media is added to this room when you capture video from your camcorder or when you import media files into your project that is already on your hard drive.

An important thing to note about adding media to your project is that the media must remain accessible to PowerDirector throughout your project. In other words, your video, stills or music must be either on your hard drive or on an external drive that is permanently attached to your computer as you edit your project. The media that appears in your **Media Room** is merely linked to the actual media files.

We'll show you how to gather media files into your **Media Room** in **Chapter 5, Start a New Project**.

The Project Room

One of the most advanced features in PowerDirector 18 Ultimate is its ability to embed projects within projects – essentially using your other editing-projects-in-progress as media in a new projects. We discuss this very cool feature in the sidebar on page 65.

The FX Room

 The **FX Room** includes a library of special effects which you can add to your video.

PowerDirector includes dozens of visual effects, all of which can be modified and customized for your particular need. For more information on the **FX Room**, see page 105.

The Video Overlay (PiP Objects) Room

 This room includes a number of cool graphics – many of them animated – which can be overlayed or added to your movie project. (For more information, see page 156.)

The **Room** also includes tools for creating your own artwork from an existing graphic or by creating animation from scratch using the **Paint Designer** workspace (see page 159).

The Particle Room

 Particles are very high level special effects, including light and lens flares, falling snow and rain, pixie dust, animated objects and cool science fiction and outer space effects – a number of which appear as three-dimensional when used in a 3D project.

As we show you on page 117, adding these dazzling animated effects to your movie is as simple as dragging them to an empty spot on your timeline (or on an upper video track so that they overlay your video).

The Title Room

The **Title Room** includes nearly 100 customizable templates for creating titles and adding text to your movie. We'll discuss this **Room** in detail in **Chapter 12**.

Media Room views

The video, still photos, music and other audio files in your **Media Room** can be viewed in a number of ways.

You'll find the options to display your media as **Details** (a list view) or **Icons** (Extra Large, Large, Medium or Small) under the **Library Menu** in the top center of the **Room**.

For more information on importing and managing media in the **Media Room**, see **Chapter 5**.

Library Menu

Get free effects and templates from the DirectorZone

The **DirectorZone** is your link to a free online community of CyberLink users. It's also a link to an amazing library of FREE PowerDirector extras.

Once you've created your account and signed in through your program, you'll have access to a huge, ever-growing library of **PiP Objects, Particles, Title Templates, DVD Menus, Magic Styles, Sounds Clips** and **Color Presets**.

For more information on joining, downloading from and uploading to the DirectorZone, see page 222 of the **Appendix**.

The Transition Room

The **Transition Room** gives you access to a huge library of video transitions, including transitions which look three-dimensional when added to a 3D project.

We'll look into this room and how to use its transitions in more detail in **Chapter 13**.

The Audio Mixing Room

The **Audio Mixing Room** includes tools for mixing the levels of your various audio tracks and for controlling your various audio levels at precise points.

We'll look at how to use the controls in this room, as well as alternative ways to control and mix your audio level sources, in **Chapter 10, Audio Editing**.

The Voice-Over Recording Room

As you'd expect, this is where you'll find the tools for recording narration into your movie. We'll look at how to use this tool in more detail on page 140.

The Chapter Room

The **Chapter Room** includes tools for adding scenes or chapters to your movie. Once these chapters have been added to your movie, the program will be able to use them to set up links on your DVD and BluRay menus that will allow your viewer to jump to specific spots in your movie.

We'll show you how to use the tools in this room to create chapters, and we'll look at the whole disc authoring process, in **Chapter 16, Disc Authoring**.

The Subtitle Room

Among the many high-level features available in PowerDirector is the ability to add optional subtitles to your movie, DVD or BluRay disc – subtitles that can be turned on and off at the viewer's discretion.

We'll look at this process in much greater depth in **Chapter 14, Add Subtitles**.

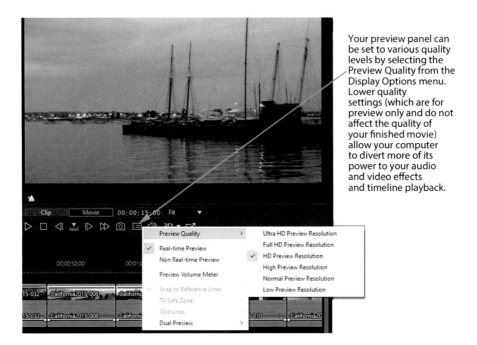

Your preview panel can be set to various quality levels by selecting the Preview Quality from the Display Options menu. Lower quality settings (which are for preview only and do not affect the quality of your finished movie) allow your computer to divert more of its power to your audio and video effects and timeline playback.

The Preview Window

The **Preview Window** displays the playback of the movie clips on your timeline.

Also, when a clip, overlay or effect is selected in the **Media Room**, this panel will show you a preview of it.

Among the settings on this panel is a menu for selecting the quality level of your video playback. This feature can be accessed by clicking on the **Preview Quality** button along the playback controls.

Higher quality playback demands more power. If your system is struggling to play your video, lowering the **Preview** quality can often smooth your video's playback.

In the event your project is still lugging your machine (i.e., if you're using several tracks of video or you've applied several video effects), you can set your playback to **Non Real-time Preview**. In **Non Real-time Preview**, the audio is muted and your video will play more slowly than normal. However, in **Non Real-time Preview** your playback will show every frame of your video at full quality.

As illustrated in the sidebar on the facing page, a toggle on the upper left of the playback controls sets the **Preview** window to play either a single, looping **Clip** on your timeline or to play your entire **Movie**.

Grab a Snapshot/Freeze Frame

Clicking the camera icon on the playback controls will grab a **Snapshot** of the frame from your movie displayed in the **Preview** window. This **Snapshot** can then be used as a freeze frame in your movie or saved for use in another program or medium. For more details on using this tool, see **How do I grab a Freeze Frame or Snapshot of my video?** on page 223.

Playback controls

The buttons along the bottom of the **Preview** window control the playback of your timeline or selected clip.

While the clip is playing, the **Play** button becomes a **Pause** button. Clicking the **Pause** button stops your movie's playback at the point of the playhead. Clicking the **Stop** button stops playback and resets it back to the beginning of your movie.

You can also play and pause your movie using the spacebar on your keyboard.

Configure your Preview for 3D Editing

If you are editing 3D video in your project, you'll want to set up your **Preview** panel to interpret and display the 3D image.

To toggle the **Preview** window into 3D mode, click on the **3D** button, as illustrated in the sidebar above. A number of 3D editing **Preview** modes will be displayed.

The most basic setting for 3D editing is **Auto Detect 3D** mode. In this mode, the program will automatically recognize the 3D footage in your project and display it accordingly.

The easiest mode for editing 3D – if you want to see the imagery in 3D as you work – is the **Anaglyph/Red-Cyan** mode. In **Anaglyph,** the right-eye and left-eye video channels are displayed as red and cyan-tinted video. If you wear red/blue 3D glasses as you work, you'll actually see the 3D video displayed as three-dimensional.

The beauty of **Anaglyph** 3D is that it requires no special TV or video equipment to display it. All you need is a pair of inexpensive red/blue glasses to view your video as 3D on any device.

PowerDirector is also capable of working with and outputting more advanced 3D video options.

For more information on editing and outputting 3D video see **Edit 3D video** beginning on page 78.

The Timeline

The **Timeline** is where your media files become a movie. The PowerDirector **Timeline** includes tracks for adding video, audio, narration, titles, effects, subtitles and disc chapter markers.

One thing worth noting about the PowerDirector timeline is that by default it's "upside-down" compared to more traditional video editing timelines. In other words, you layer video from the top track down rather than from the bottom track up. Video on **Video 2** will appear overlayed on top of the video on **Video 1**, despite that fact that is *underneath* it on the **Timeline** itself. Since version 18, however, this configuration can be reversed, as discussed on page 12.

The PowerDirector **Timeline** is made up of several tracks, some of which can be optionally hidden. To display, hide or add tracks, **right-click** on one of the track headers on the left.

A Chapter track (optional), for adding DVD and BluRay chapters to your movie, discussed in **Chapter 16**.

A Subtitle track (optional), for adding subtitles to your movie, discussed in **Chapter 14**.

A Clip Marker track (optional), for pacing your movie to music, discussed in **Chapter 10**.

Video tracks, on which you can place video, still photos, graphics or titles.

Audio tracks, on which you can place music or other audio.

An FX track, on which video effects can be added to your movie. (In PowerDirector, video effects can be added directly to a clip on your timeline or to this separate track, in which case the effect works as an adjustment layer, the effect applied to every video paired with it on **Video 1**.)

A Title track (although titles can also be added to any video track) as discussed in **Chapter 12.**

A Voice-over track, to which any voice-overs are recorded into your project.

A Music track (although any audio can be added to this track, and music can be added to any audio track).

Additional video and audio tracks can be added to your timeline as needed – up to 100 additional video and 98 additional audio tracks. (See **Tell stories with multiple video tracks** on page 155.)

To add video and audio tracks, click the **Add Tracks** button on the top left of the Timeline or simply **right-click** on an empty spot on the **Timeline** and select the option.

Clips on a track can be locked into place by clicking the **Padlock** icon on the track header, to the left of the timeline, as illustrated at the top of the facing page.

Audio and video tracks can also be temporarily disabled (made invisible or muted) by unchecking the checkbox on the track header.

Custom name your Timeline tracks

Your PowerDirector **Timeline** tracks have, by default, generic names. (If you can't see these track names, widen the track header column by dragging the seam between the track headers and the main timeline.)

To custom name a track, simply click on the generic track name and type over it.

Drag on the seam to widen Track Header and display track names.

Re-order your Timeline tracks

Your video tracks are displayed as a stack, with the higher-numbered tracks (which appear by default lower on the **Timeline**) appearing "on top of" the lower-numbered tracks in your movie.

To change the stacking order of your tracks, click on the track header and drag it above or below other tracks. (The track numbering will automatically update.)

Zoom in and out of your timeline

Sometimes you want to step back and see much or all of your movie at once. Other times you want to zoom in on a single clip or individual frame.

To zoom in or out, adjust the slider in the lower left of the **Timeline** or click its **+** or **-** buttons.

Alternatively, you can zoom out or in by clicking and dragging over the timecode "ticker" along the top of the **Timeline**.

Widen or narrow your timeline

If you're working on a high-level video with lots of effects and video and audio tracks, you may find that the **Timeline** gets pretty crowded pretty quickly.

There are a couple of things you can do to streamline this workspace.

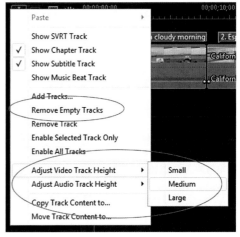

- **Remove empty tracks**. **Right-click** anywhere on your timeline and you'll find the option to **Remove Empty Tracks**. This strips your timeline view down to only the tracks that you're actually using.

- **Adjust your tracks' heights**. **Right-click** on any track on your timeline and you'll find the option to change your track's height. The track heights can be displayed as Small, Medium or Large.

Reversing the
Timeline track order

Reverse the order of the tracks on the Timeline

A long-time "eccentricity" unique to PowerDirector is that, unlike virtually every other video editor, its **Timeline** is by default upside down.

In other words, **Video 1** (the bottom track) is at the top of the **Timeline**, while the tracks overlaying it (**Video 2, Video 3, Video 4**) are displayed below it. When you add a video or title that will appear over your main video, you place it on a track *below* that video on the **Timeline**.

Some people find this a bit counter-intuitive.

If you'd prefer, you can set the program to display your video and audio tracks from bottom to top. **Video 1** (the main or bottom video track) will appear at the bottom of the **Timeline**, while the overlaying tracks will appear above.

To reverse the track listings on the **Timeline**, go to the program's **Preferences** (by clicking on the **Cog** at the top of the program) and, on **Editing** page, check **Reverse Timeline Track Order (Track 1 at Bottom)**.

Undock the program's windows

If you have a dual-monitor set-up on your computer or you just have a really large screen and you'd like to spread the program out, you can undock the various windows and rooms and scatter them around your desktop.

To make any window locked to the interface a separate, floating window, right-click anywhere within the panel and select the option to **Dock/Undock Window.**

To place the window back into the program's interface, right-click anywhere in the window and select **Dock/Undock Window**. The panel will re-appear in its default location.

Media is either captured from a device or imported into your project from your hard drive.

Basic editing moves

No matter what you plan to do with your video and no matter how creatively you plan to do it, the video editing process itself will still fit the same basic structure.

Here's a brief walkthrough of the basic steps you'll take creating a video project in PowerDirector.

1 ### Gather your media

The assets, or media, you gather to create your movie can come from a variety of sources. It can be video, audio, music, photos or graphics. It can be from a tape-based HDV or miniDV camcorder or web cam, from a hard drive or storage camcorder (such as an AVCHD camcorder), from a smartphone or other recording device, from a live TV signal or from a DVD or CD.

To get your media from a camcorder, recording device or disc, go to the **Capture** workspace by selecting it from the program's **File** menu (or by pressing **Alt+F9** on your keyboard).

In the **Capture** workspace, you'll find options for interfacing with these devices. Once you've selected the appropriate tool, set the location the media will be captured to and properly configured your connection to your device, you'll stream or copy the video or other media onto your hard drive and into your project. Your media files will be automatically added to your project's **Media Room**.

If your video, still photos, music or other audio files are already on your hard drive, you merely need to import them into your project's **Media Room**.

To import media into your project, click the **Import Media** button at the top left of the **Media Room** and browse to the media files you'd like to add to your project.

For more information on starting a PowerDirector project and gathering media, see **Chapter 5, Start a New Project**.

Trim your clips to remove video from the beginning or end.
Split clips to slice through your clips at the position of the playhead.

2 Assemble the clips on your timeline

Once you've imported your media clips into a project, you can begin the process of assembling your movie.

PowerDirector offers two views for your timeline: The more traditional **Timeline** view and the quick-assembly **Storyboard** view. You can switch between these views by selecting the option under the program's **View** menu or by pressing the **Tab** button on your keyboard. We'll look at assembling your movie in either view in **Chapter 6, Gather Media on the Timeline**.

Clips are added to your timeline by dragging them from the **Media Room** to a position on the **Timeline**.

When a clip is dragged onto or will overlap an existing clip on your timeline, a pop-up menu will offer you the option of overlaying the existing clip or splitting it and inserting the new clip into your movie, rippling the rest of the timeline aside to accommodate it.

Once your video or audio clips are added to your timeline, you can begin the process of actually editing your movie clips:

Trim your clips. Trimming means removing footage from either the beginning or the end of a clip. To trim a clip, click to select the clip on your timeline and then drag in either the beginning or end to shorten it, as in the illustration above.

Split your clips. Splitting means slicing through your clips so that you can remove footage from the middle or delete one sliced-off segment completely. To split a clip, position the playhead over a selected clip, at the point where you'd like the split to happen, then click the **Split** button along the top of the **Timeline**.

Place your clip on upper video or audio track. The use of multiple tracks of video is the key to the creation of many of the more advanced video effects, including **Chroma Key** (see page 109) and **Picture-in-Picture** effects (see **Chapter 11**).

PowerDirector includes many options for enhancing or adding effects to your movies.

3 Add and adjust effects

CyberLink PowerDirector comes loaded with a library of professional effects for adding magic to your movies – everything from fixes, like color adjustments and video stabilizers, to cool visual effects for stylizing the look of your movie, to **Particle** tools for creating snow and rain effects.

Adding and customizing effects for your movie is fun and easy, as we show you in **Chapter 9, Video Effects and Animations**.

When a clip is selected on your timeline, a number of **Function Buttons** will appear along the top of the **Timeline**. Depending on the properties of the clip you have selected, these **Function Buttons** may include:

Tools offers access to the **PiP Designer, Mask Designer, View Designer, Action Cam Designer, Crop/Zoom/Pan, Video Speed, Video in Reverse, Motion Tracker, Blending Modes** and **Content Aware Editing**. These workspaces include tools for adding effects, creating fade ins and fade outs, for cutting your video into various shapes and for designating specific views on a 360° clip. Under this button you'll also find access to tools for editing and mixing your movie's audio.

Fix/Enhance offers access to tools for correcting your video clip's lighting or color as well as for stabilizing, or taking the shake out of your videos. Additionally, the library of **Color Effects** tools available in this panel allows you to change the mood or color tone of a sequence with a single click (as we show you on page 102).

Keyframe offers access to a number of tools for creating special effects and animations and for controlling levels of audio and video that vary over the course of a clip.

Among the unique effects available in PowerDirector is the ability to make your 2D video into a 3D movie (see page 79). And it's remarkably effective!

To apply a transition, drag it from the Transition Room onto the intersection of two clips on your timeline.

4 Add and adjust transitions

Transitions are the effects or animations that take your movie from one clip to another. Some are subtle and nearly invisible – others are showy and draw attention to themselves. Transitions, like effects, can be added to your timeline and customized to fit your needs:

1 **Select the Transition Room** from the tabs that run along the top left side of the interface.

2 **Apply a transition.**

Apply a transition by dragging it from the **Transition Room** onto the intersection of two clips on your timeline.

We'll discuss transitions and how to work with them in greater detail in **Chapter 13.**

5 Add titles

Titles are text, and sometimes graphics, placed over your clips to provide additional visual information for your video story. You can choose an existing template, or create a custom title in the **Title Designer.**

1 **Select the Title Room** from the tabs that run along the left side of the interface.

Once a title is added to your timeline, you can customize it in the Title Designer.

2 Add the title to your timeline.

Drag a selected title template to your timeline, on a track below the video you'd like it to appear over.

3 Customize your title's look.

Double-click the title on your timeline. This will open the **Title Designer**, in which you can set your text's color, font and style as well as select a **Motion** animation.

We'll show you how to create and customize your titles in **Chapter 12, Add Text and Titles**.

 Produce your movie

When you're happy with the video project you've created, you'll find a number of options for publishing and sharing it, as we discuss in **Section 4** of this book. We'll show you how to publish it as a:

- **Computer file.** Create an AVI, MPEG, AVC, WMV, MP4 or MKV in standard or 3D format!
- **Device file.** Create a video for your smartphone, Apple, Sony or Microsoft device, or send it back to your camcorder for archiving.
- **Web file.** Load your finished video directly to YouTube, Daily Motion, Vimeo, Niconico or Youku.
- **Disc.** PowerDirector includes tools for adding chapter markers, creating disc menus and authoring your DVD or BluRay disc.

And that's basically it!

You gather your assets; you assemble them on your timeline; you add effects, transitions and titles; then you share your masterpiece with the world.

But between the lines of this simplicity are the countless variations that can elevate your movie project from the realm of a basic structure to something truly amazing!

And that's, of course, what this book is all about.

What's new in CyberLink PowerDirector 19?

CyberLink continues to refine its already excellent video editor with some nice new features.

In the latest version of PowerDirector, CyberLink has refined the interface and made a number of tools easier to access. You'll also find new effects and templates throughout the program as well as a number of new and enhanced Designer workspaces.

Custom animated mask designer

In addition to tools for using mask templates or creating masks based on text, the **Mask Designer** now includes a tool for creating vector-based custom masks. The mask can be drawn in any shape – to track with a person or object in your video, for instance – and then animated to move and even change shape over the course of your video.

We show you how to use this very cool tool on page 125 of **Chapter 9, Video Effects and Animations**.

Motion graphic titles

In addition to its library of stationary and animated title templates, the **Titles Room** now includes templates that use animated text and graphics. These elements can even be customized, and the graphic elements custom-colored.

We show you how to customize those motion graphics titles on page 172 of **Chapter 12, Add Text and Titles**.

Sketch Animations

New to the **Video Overlay (PiP Objects) Room** library are **Sketch Animations**, animated arrows, circles and other graphics that appear to be hand-drawn in real time over your videos!

These animations can be customized in a number of ways. We show you how to add a custom color and how to control the speed of their animation on page 164 of **Chapter 11, PiPs and Multi-Track Video Effects**.

Upgraded Screen Recorder

CyberLink has also upgraded one of PowerDirector's best bonus tools, its built-in **Screen Recorder**.

The **Screen Recorder** now includes options for recording narration live, and for adding a webcam inset of yourself narrating your tutorial or game. Webcam capture even includes a Chroma Key feature so you can add custom "fake" backgrounds to your webcam videos!

We show you how to use this very advanced tool beginning on page 50 of **Chapter 5, Start a New Project**.

Need some Basic Training?

Want some help with the basics of CyberLink PowerDirector?

Want some free hands-on training?

Check out my free tutorial series **Basic Training for CyberLink PowerDirector** at Muvipix.com.

This simple, eight-part series will show you how to set up a project, how to import media into it, basic editing moves, adding transitions and effects, how to create titles and how to export your finished video.

And did I mention that it's free?

To see the series, just go to Muvipix.com/cpd19.php or look up Basic Training for CyberLink PowerDirector on YouTube.

And while you're on our site, why not drop by the Community forum and say hi! We'd love to have you become a part of our growing community. Happy moviemaking!

Steve, Chuck, Ron and the whole Muvipix team

Section 2

Easy Editing Modes

The Movie Magic Wizard

Easy Editor Styles

Adjustments and Editing

The Theme Designer

Chapter 2

Make Simple Movies in Auto Mode

Instant Moviemaking

Auto Mode in CyberLink PowerDirector is a quick and easy way to produce movies from your video clips.

PowerDirector's Magic Movie Wizard automatically adds the effects, titles, music and fun!

To create a Magic Movie, select the Auto Mode on the Welcome Screen.

Be sure to also select your movie's Aspect Ratio!

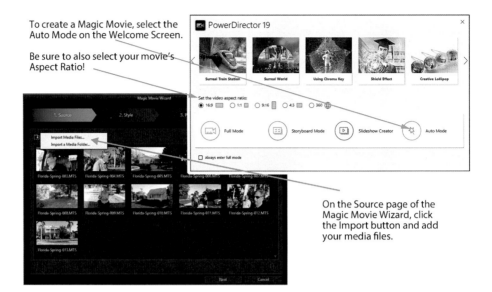

On the Source page of the Magic Movie Wizard, click the Import button and add your media files.

The **Magic Movie Wizard** is a semi-automatic workspace for making your movies. You supply the raw footage or photos; you pick the style of movie; you customize its look and feel – and the **Magic Movie Wizard** does the rest!

1 Select Auto Mode

At the program's **Welcome Screen**, set the **Aspect Ratio** to either 4:3, widescreen 16:9, portrait 9:16 or square 1:1 and click the **Auto Mode** button.

The **Magic Movie Wizard** can also be launched from within a project, under the **Plugins** menu in the **Editing** workspace.

The **Magic Movie Wizard** will open.

2 Import your media

On the **Source** page of the **Magic Movie Wizard**, click the **Import Your Videos and Photos** button.

You have the option of importing individual photos or video clips or importing an entire folder of media files.

Click **Next**.

3 Select a Magic Style

Select a **Style** for your movie, as illustrated on the facing page. Note that some styles are indicated as 3D. These styles should be used if you're editing a 3D movie. If you're signed in to the **DirectorZone** (see page 222), you can download additional **Magic Styles** by clicking the **Free Download** button.

To customize the music, audio mix and duration of your movie, click the **Settings** button in the lower left of this panel. Or, to proceed directly to your movie's preview, click **Next**. (Go to **Step 6**.)

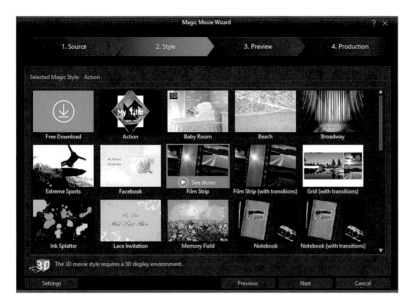

4   Adjust music, audio and duration Settings

On the **Settings** panel, (illustrated below) click the music button to add **Background Music** to your movie.

Use the **Audio Level** slider to adjust if the background music or video sound dominates your movie – or slide it all the way to the right to include only music in your movie.

By default, your movie will be as long as your music or video files (whichever is longer). However, you can select the option to make your movie only as long as your music or set it to a custom duration by using the controls under **Specify the Movie Duration**.

5 **Adjust Advanced Settings**

Click the **Advanced Settings** button at the bottom of the **Magic Movie Wizard** to customize how the Wizard uses your video or photos.

Click **OK** to close the **Advanced Settings**, then click **Next**.

The Wizard will analyze your clips and create a **Preview** of your movie.

6 **Preview and tweak your movie**

Once the Wizard has created a **Preview** of your movie, you can tweak it.

Add Media or Effects.   Select Visual Template.   Customize title(s).

7   Edit your Theme

To customize your movie's template, click the **Edit In The Theme** button along the bottom of the **Preview** page.

A **Theme Designer** will open in which you can add or modify your effects, add titles over individual sequences, change the music and even mute individual clips.

Type in a custom **Title**.

8   Finish your movie

Once you're satisfied with your adjustments, click **OK** to close the Theme Designer, then click **Next** at the bottom of the Preview page.

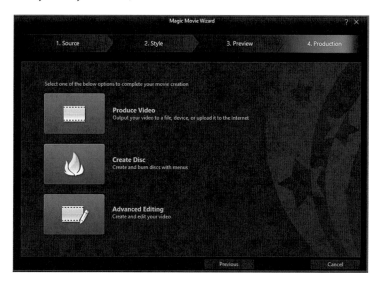

You'll be taken to the **Production** page, from which you can output your movie as a video file, upload it to a Web site, create a DVD or BluRay disc or send the file to **Full Feature Editing** for further tweaking.

The Slideshow Creator

Styles & Music

Customizing Your Slideshow

Chapter 3

Create Slideshows with the Slideshow Creator

Giving Life to Your Still Photos

A good slideshow can give life to your still photos. It adds movement, adds focus and piques the viewer's interest in a way a mere photo can not.

PowerDirector includes great semi-automatic ways for building and sharing your slideshows.

To create a slideshow, select the Slideshow Creator option on the Welcome Screen.

Be sure to also select your movie's Aspect Ratio.

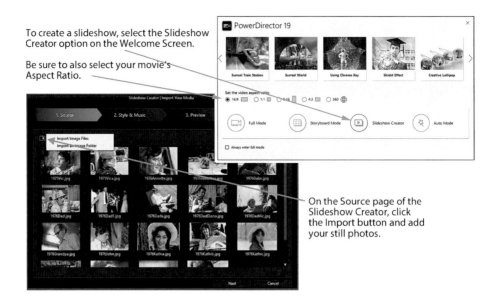

On the Source page of the Slideshow Creator, click the Import button and add your still photos.

Although you can build your slideshows in the **Full Featured Editor**, simply by dragging your photos to the project's timeline, PowerDirector includes an easy-to-use tool for creating great-looking slideshows practically automatically.

1   Select the Slideshow Creator

At the program's **Welcome Screen**, set the **Aspect Ratio** to 4:3, widescreen 16:9, portrait 9:16 or square 1:1.

Click the **Slideshow Creator** button.

The **Slideshow Creator** Wizard will open.

2   Import your media

On the **Source** page of the **Slideshow Creator**, click the **Import Your Photos** button.

You'll have the option of importing individual image files or importing an entire folder of image files at once.

Click **Next**.

3   Select a Style & Music

Select a **Style** for your movie, as illustrated on the facing page. Note that some styles are indicated as 3D button.

 Click the **Select Background Music** button to add music to your slideshow.

Click the **Slideshow Preferences** button to set whether the slideshow duration is set by your music or photo length.

Click the **Music Preferences** button to trim your music's in and out points and to add a fade in or fade out to your music.

Click **OK** to close the window, then click **Next**.

The **Slideshow Creator** will build a **Preview** of your slideshow.

4   Preview your movie

If you're happy with the results, click **Next**.

5 Tweak your Slideshow

Many templates include the option to **Customize** or **Replace Background**. Click on the button in the lower left of the **Preview** panel to open the **Slideshow Designer**.

In the **Slideshow Designer**, you may find options for customizing your slideshow's look or setting the number of photos to appear on each slide.

Click **OK** to close the window, then click **Next**.

6 Finish your movie

You'll be taken to the **Production** page, from which you can output your movie as a video file, upload it to a Web site, create a DVD or BluRay disc or send the file to **Full Feature Editing** for further tweaking.

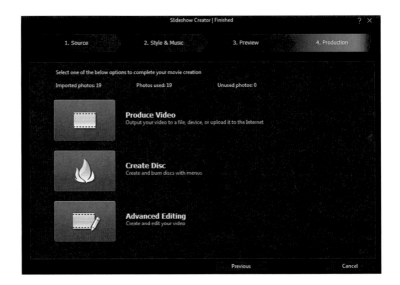

Cool Slideshow Styles

The PowerDirector **Slideshow Creator** also includes a number of very cool styles. Here are a couple of my personal favorites.

Frozen Space creates a slideshow in which your photos seem to float around in space.

Motion automatically adds pans and zooms and transitions to your slideshow.

Time-Lapse Slideshow. This cool style creates a slideshow in which you can designate the length of each slide's duration – making it ideal for creating time-lapse videos in which, say, a camera snaps a picture every five seconds. Clicking the **Customize** button on the **Preview** page opens the option panel for setting your slides' durations.

Balloon and **Outer Space styles** create your slideshows as very cool stereoscopic 3D movies.

Frozen Space

Stereoscopic 3D Outer Space

Time-Lapse with option screen

Section 3

Full Feature Editing

Using Express Project Templates

Replacing Placeholders with Video

Customizing Your Titles

Chapter 4

Make an Express Project
Building your movies from templates

PowerDirector Express Projects is a library of templates that you can use to build exciting movie sequences – complete with titles, transitions and effects – by simply dragging your video clips into timeline placeholders.

It's a bit more hands-on than Auto Mode's Magic Movie Wizard, with more customizable features.

To create an Express Project, select the Full Mode or Storyboard Mode option on the Welcome Screen.

Be sure to also select your movie's Aspect Ratio.

In the Editing workspace, select the Express Projects category in the Project Room.

PowerDirector's **Express Project** tool helps you build exciting sequences for your movies by providing pre-designed templates for openings, middles and endings, complete with effects, transitions and cool animated titles.

To access this library of templates, open PowerDirector in either **Full Mode** or **Storyboard Mode** and, in the **Project Room**, select the **Express Projects** category**.** You can also open the **Express Project** library by selecting the option under the **Plugins** menu.

1   **Select an Express Project template**

The **Project Room** will display the library of **Express Project** templates.

The **Express Project** library will display templates for creating openings, middles or ending sequences for your movie. These sequence templates are arranged by subject, including **Sports, Travel** and **Weddings**. If you click the **Free Templates** button in the upper left of the panel, you'll be connected to the **Director Zone**, where you can access a huge library of additional free **Express Project** templates, many created by fellow users. (For more information on the **DirectorZone**, see page 222.)

2   **Add a template to your timeline**

Drag a template from the **Media Room** to **Video Track 1** on your timeline.

Because templates usually include effects and titles, the template will spread over a number of video and effects tracks. The template is composed of placeholders which will eventually be replaced by your own video.

You can preview your **Express Project** template or your movie-in-progress at any time simply by playing your movie's timeline.

The Express Project library includes templates for openings, middles and endings in a number of categories..

When added to your timeline, the template will add transitions, effects and titles and video clip placeholders.

3 Locate your project's media

To replace the template placeholders with your video clips, open the **Media Room** by clicking the button in the top left of the interface. If you haven't yet gathered the video you plan to use in your project, import your media into your project (as described in **Chapter 5**).

4 Replace the Express Project placeholders

Your **Express Project** video clip placeholders will appear on your timeline as black clips with the numbers 1, 2, 3, etc., on them.

To replace a placeholder with a video clip, drag your video clip from the **Media Room** directly onto the placeholder.

The video clip will replace the placeholder and any effects or transitions that were applied to the placeholder will appear on the clip. (If a menu appears offering to overlay your video over the placeholder, you haven't dragged your clip directly *onto* the placeholder.)

Gather your media in the Media Room.

Drag your media files down onto the placeholders. As they replace each placeholder, the video clips will pick up the placeholder's effects and transitions.

Double-click any template title to open them in the Title Designer where you can customize the text and, if you'd like, add effects and transitions.

5 Customize your titles

Locate any **Express Project** titles on your timeline.

To customize the text on a title, **double-click** on it. The title will open in the **Title Designer**.

Select and overwrite any text blocks in the title. (For more information on the **Title Designer**, see **Chapter 12, Add Titles**.)

Express Project templates are a simple way to build exciting effects and animated titles into your movie.

The effects and titles can be used as is or you can customize the individual elements any way you'd like using the tools in the **Full Feature Editor**.

The Welcome Screen

Capturing Video from a Tape-based Camcorder

Getting Video from an AVCHD Camcorder or Device

Ripping Media from Discs

Recording Your Computer Screen

Importing Media into Your Project

Configuring Your Project Settings

Chapter 5
Start a New Project
Smart beginnings

No matter how great the journey ahead, it all begins with a few key steps in the right direction.

And, no matter how simple or how complicated your movie project is, a good start can go a long way toward ensuring a successful editing experience.

Aspect Ratio

PowerDirector does a great job of analyzing your source video and setting up its project to match your video's specs.

About all you need to do is select an **Aspect Ratio** for your video frame. PowerDirector 19 includes options for setting up your project as **4:3** (the old TV format), **16:9 widescreen**, **9:16 portrait** (the aspect ratio your smartphone shoots at if you hold it upright rather than sideways) and even **square 1:1**, for online sites like Instagram, YouTube, Vimeo and Facebook. (For information on further configuring your project's settings, see page 53.)

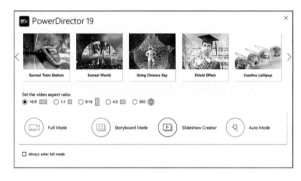

Additionally, PowerDirector can be set to edit **360° video,** a format (sometimes called VR) which records the entire 360° scene surrounding the camera. The movie's viewer can then select where in that scene he or she looks. For more information on **360° video** editing, see page 81.

Additionally, when editing higher definition video, the program can utilize **shadow files** (see page 224) to make your ultra high-def editing experience as efficient as possible.

Start a new project

There are several ways to start a project in CyberLink PowerDirector:

- Select an **Editing** mode from the **Welcome Screen**.

  From this **Welcome Screen**, you will find options to open the program in **Timeline Mode (Full Mode), Storyboard Mode** (see page 75) or **Auto Mode** (see **Chapter 2**), or to open the **Slideshow Creator** (**Chapter 3**) or the **360° Video Editor** (see page 81).

- In **Full Mode** or **Storyboard Mode**, select **New Project** from the **File** menu.

- In **Full Mode** or **Storyboard Mode**, press **Ctrl+n** on your keyboard.

Open into a project in progress?

By default, PowerDirector will open into a new, blank project.

If you'd rather the program open into your most recent work in progress, you can set this option on the **Project** page of your **Preferences**, launched by clicking the **Cog** icon at the top of the interface.

Note that you can select the option to skip the **Welcome Screen** and go directly into a **Full Mode** project by checking the box in the lower left of this screen.

Add media to your project

CyberLink PowerDirector Ultimate will work with a large number of media formats.

Video: 3GPP2, Microsoft AVI, DAT, DV-AVI, DVR-MS, FLV, M2T and MTS, MKV, MOD, MOV (H.264, HEVC H.265 and Apple ProRes 10-bit), MP4 (H.264 and HEVC H.265), MPEG (standard and high-definition), MTS, MXF 8-bit 420 AVC, TOD, WEBM, MP4 (including MP4s using the new HEVC/H.265 codec), VOB (DVD video) VRO, WMV and XAVC-S 4K video. Additionally, PowerDirector can edit the dual-stream AVI, MVC and MKV 3D video formats.

Still Photos: BMP, GIF, Apple HEIC, JPEG, PNG, TIFF, RAW, Animated GIF and 3D JPS and MPO.

Audio: ALAC, FLAC, M4A, MP3, OGG, WAV and WMA.

How your media is added to your project depends on where the files are located – and if they need to be captured or downloaded from a camcorder or other recording device. **All media files used in your projects must be stored on your computer's hard drive and always accessible to the program**. If you disconnect a device on which your media files are stored, the program will no longer be able to use its link to these video or audio files to edit and create your project. In other words, you need to copy your video from your camcorder to your computer.

Capture video from a miniDV or HDV camcorder

Capturing video means gathering your video from a device in real time. Real-time capture means that you essentially record the digital video stream as your camcorder plays it or it streams in live.

Devices that PowerDirector can capture streams of video from include:

A **miniDV** or **HDV** (high-definition) tape-based camcorder.
A **live TV** or **Digital TV** signal or a **Webcam** or a **microphone** (see page 49 for more details).

To capture tape-based or live video:

1   **Open the Capture workspace**

Select **Capture** from the program's **File** menu or press **Alt+F9**.

The **Capture** workspace will open and, if your camcorder is connected by an IEEE-1394 (FireWire) connection or your TV signal or Webcam is receiving a signal, its corresponding **Capture** tab will be highlighted.

MiniDV camcorder capture
HDV camcorder capture

2   **Select your device**

Your video will be displayed in the **Capture Preview** window.

Click PowerDirector's playback controls to play and cue up your tape.

3   **Select your Capture Profile and location**

Click the **Profile** button in the lower right of the **Capture** workspace.

If you are capturing video from a miniDV camcorder, select the **AVI/DV** format.

If you are capturing high-definition or HDV video, you should select the **MPEG2** or **H.264** format – although, for some devices, the program will make this selection for you.

Click the **Change Folder** button (illustrated at the top of this page) to select where on your computer your captured video will be saved.

4   **Set Capture Preferences**

Click the **Cog** at the top of the interface to open **Preferences** and go to **Capture**.

On this page, you can opt to have the program break your captured video by scenes, based on your camcorder's timecode.

5   **Begin your capture**

To begin capture, cue your tape (if you're capturing from a camcorder) to the spot you'd like capture to begin, and click the **Capture** (red dot) button.

The video will be recorded to your computer's hard drive as the video data is streamed in and displayed in the **Preview** window.

To end your capture, click **Pause** or **Stop.**

To edit your video, select **Edit** from the program's **File** menu or press **Alt+F10**.

Batch Capture your tape-based video

The biggest challenge to capturing tape-based video in real time is that you have to pretty much sit next to your computer and wait for the video to stream in.

PowerDirector includes two **Batch Capture** modes that the program can use to do the actual capturing automatically, based on parameters you've set.

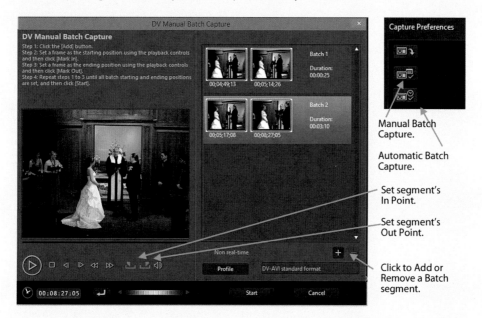

Manual Batch Capture.

Automatic Batch Capture.

Set segment's In Point.

Set segment's Out Point.

Click to Add or Remove a Batch segment.

Manual Batch Capture

When you select **Manual Batch Capture**, the program will open up into a workspace in which you can set where on your tape you'd like your video captures to begin and end. You can set up several of these segments (which is why it's called "batch" capture).

To add a batch capture segment, click the **+** button in the lower right of the panel.

To set a beginning for a segment, use the playback controls to cue your tape, then click the **In Point** button. To set where you'd like your capture to end, re-cue your tape and click the **Out Point** button. Use **+** to add as many **In** and **Out Points** as you'd like.

When you've set all of your **In** and **Out Points**, click the **Start** button – then go grab a cup of coffee while the program does the actual capturing for you.

Automatic Batch Capture

When you select **Automatic Batch Capture**, the program will ask you to rewind your camcorder to the beginning of your tape. When you click the **Start** button, the program will capture your tape, breaking your captured video into scenes, based on the tape's timecode, wherever you've paused or stopped your camcorder's recording.

Import video from AVCHD camcorders, smartphones and other video recording devices

In order to use your video or other media in a PowerDirector project, this media must ultimately be on your computer's hard drive or on an external drive that is permanently connected to your computer. This is because your PowerDirector project will link to these media files, and they must be available to the program whenever you edit your movie.

In short, your first step in gathering your video and audio assets for a project is to get this media from your camcorder or other device to your computer.

There are actually a couple of ways to get video from camcorders (including smartphones, iPads, etc.) that store video on an internal hard drive or SD card.

The most common way to get your video or audio from an external device is to simply copy the video and/or audio files to your computer using your computer's operating system and then import this media into your project, as discussed in **Import video and audio already on your hard drive** on page 52.

To copy your video files from a camcorder or other recording device to your computer, connect your camcorder to your computer with a USB cable and then open Windows' File Explorer.

Your camcorder will need to be turned on and in **VTR/Play** mode. Many camcorders will also require you to have your camcorder plugged into an AC outlet and some may need some additional configuration in order to interface with your computer.

1   **Browse to the camcorder's video storage**

In Windows File Explorer your device will be displayed under **Computer** as either a **Hard Disk Drive** or **Portable Device**.

Double-click on the device listing.

As illustrated on the facing page, you'll likely need to browse down through a number of folders to find the video files, which are usually in the form of .mts, .mp4 or sometimes .mov files.

2   **Copy your files**

Select the files you want to copy by clicking while holding down the **Shift** key (to select several in a sequence) or the **Ctrl** key (to select several individually).

Right-click on the selected files and select **Cut** or **Copy**.

3 **Paste to your computer**

Browse to the location on your computer's drive you'd like to add your files to, **right-click** and select **Paste**. The files will be copied or transferred to this location.

4 **Import the files into your project**

In PowerDirector's **Edit** workspace, click the **Import** button at the top of the **Media Room** and select **Import Media Files** – then browse to and select your video files. Click **Open**.

The files will be added to your project's **Media Room** library.

Capture video or audio live from a Webcam, microphone or TV tuner

If your computer includes a TV Tuner card or Webcam or you have a microphone plugged into your computer, you can capture the audio and/or video live from this device.

1 **Select your device**

Select **Capture** from the program's **File** menu or press **Alt+F9**.

In the **Capture** workspace, select your device or tuner card from the options highlighted along the top of the **Capture** window, illustrated at the top of page 48.

Webcam
Microphone
CD and DVD or other device
TV or a Digital TV tuner

Select the device from the top of the Capture Preview window.

Click the Settings button to set your capture preferences.

Set where you'd like your media to be captured to.

Click the Capture button.

2   **Set Capture Preferences**

Click the **Settings** button in the lower right of the **Capture** workspace. Set your capture's resolution and parameters, as illustrated above.

To set where your captured video files are saved, click the **Change Folder** button.

3   **Click Capture**

When you click the red **Capture** button, your live feed will be recorded to your computer and added to your PowerDirector project.

To edit your video, select **Edit** from the program's **File** menu or press **Alt+F10**.

Rip video or audio from a CD, DVD or BluRay disc

To copy video from a disc, place the CD, DVD or BluRay disc in your computer's disk drive and use the method described in **Import Video Files from AVCHD Camcorders** on page 47.

Note that most *commercial* DVDs and BluRays include copy protection software that will block you from copying these discs.

If your disc is from a DVD camcorder, ensure that the disc is **finalized** before placing it in your computer's disk drive.

Select the External or Optical Drive option.

Preview your disc, select which movies you want to capture and then click the red Record button.

Set where your files are recorded to.

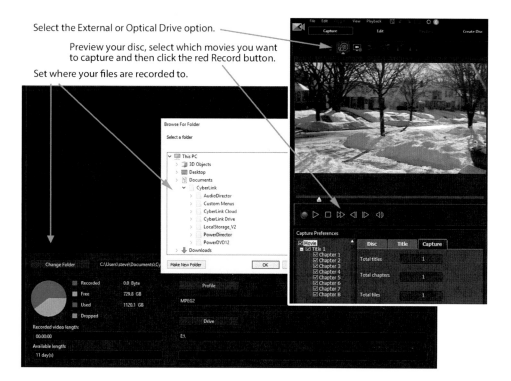

1   **Open the Capture workspace**

Select **Capture** from the program's **File** menu or press **Alt+F9**.

With your CD, DVD or BluRay in your computer's disk drive, click the **Capture** button at the top left of the interface.

The **Capture from External or Optical Device** tab should be highlighted along the top of the **Capture Preview** window.

2   **Set your Capture Preferences**

Click the **Change Folder** button in the lower right of the interface to select where you'd like your video saved on your hard drive. Your video will be saved as MPEG2 files.

In the box below the **Capture Preview** window, check which of the clips on your camcorder you'd like to capture.

You can preview the clips using the playback buttons on the **Capture Preview** window.

4   **Click Capture**

When you click the red **Capture** button, your selected video files will be copied to your computer and added to your PowerDirector project.

To edit your video, select **Edit** from the program's **File** menu or press **Alt+F10**.

Record your computer screen

A terrific bonus feature included with PowerDirector 19 is a very nice screen recording app – actually built right into the program. The video and audio recorded from your computer (including your own voiceover, if you've got a microphone attached) are saved in a fully editable format – or, if you'd prefer, in a format you can upload directly to a social media site like YouTube.

This is a great tool for, say, recording tutorials or recording demonstrations of software, games or web browsing.

1   **Open the Screen Recorder**

Select **Capture** from the program's **File** menu or press **Alt+F9**. In the **Capture** workspace, click the **Record from Screen** button.

The program will minimize and the **Screen Recorder** control panel will open, as illustrated above.

2   **Select your recording parameters**

The app included with PowerDirector 19 can be set to record your **Full Screen**, to record a **Game** or program demonstration, or to record live-capture a **Device** like a USB-connected web cam. It can be **Locked to an App**, in which case it will automatically size itself to the program or window you select. Or you can select the **Custom** option, in which case you can size the capture window to your own personal preference. (More options are available if you purchase the upgraded version of the app.) The area to be captured will appear on your monitor surrounded by a yellow dotted line.

The recorder can be set to record your screen at 1080p, 720p or 480p at either the traditional 30 frames per second or at a number of frame rates from 15 to 120 fps.

Along the bottom of the **Screen Recorder** panel you will find options for adding your **Webcam** as a custom-sizable inset for your screen capture, for recording your **Microphone** and for adding a graphic or **Video Overlay**.

A cool feature included with the latest version of this app is the ability to add a custom background to your webcam capture using live **Chroma Key**. To use this feature, click on **Cog** at the top right of the **Screen Recorder** panel and, on the preferences panel that opens, select the **Webcam** preferences page.

When you check the **Chroma Key** option, a preview of your webcam view will be displayed and you'll be prompted to select a color or color range in your background to replace, similar to using the **Chroma Key** effect described on page 109. You can then browse to a new **Background** the clicking the option at the bottom of this preferences page.

As with any **Chroma Key effect**, you'll get the best results if your original webcam background is smooth and evenly-colored, ideally a blue or green screen or wall.

3   **Record your screen**

Once you've selected the area of your screen you want to capture, click the red **REC** button on the Screen Recorder panel or press the **F9** key.

The **Screen Recorder** will minimize and, after a three-second countdown, the app will begin recording.

4   **Pause or stop your recording**

To pause your recording, press **F10** on your keyboard.

To finish and save your recording, press **F9**.

Once you stop recording, the app will close and you will be returned to the PowerDirector **Capture** workspace. A Windows File Explorer browse screen will open, indicating the location of your captured video.

These MP4 files can be viewed or shared to social media as is or they can be edited in PowerDirector 19.

To edit your captured video, switch PowerDirector to its **Edit** workspace (by selecting **Edit** from the program's **File** menu) and then drag the video file from Windows File Explorer to the **Media Room** or directly to the **Timeline**.

Import video and audio files already on your hard drive

To add video, photos, music and other audio files that are already on your computer to your project, you will need to import them into your project.

In the **Edit** workspace, click the **Import** button at the top of the **Media Room**, select the option to either **Import Media Files** or **Import a Media Folder** and browse to and select your media files. Then click **Open**.

The imported media will appear in your **Media Room**.

As you can see in the illustration above, you also have options for downloading media from your **CyberLink Cloud** (see page 226) or the CyberLink **DirectorZone** (as discussed on page 222).

Indicating 3D video

PowerDirector does a great job of automatically assimilating and interpreting whatever video you add to it. However, it's a good idea to "advise" the program when you've added a 3D clip (even if you plan to use it in a 2D project).

To set these preferences, **right-click** on the clip in your **Media Room** (or on the **Timeline**) and select the option to **Set 3D Source Format**.

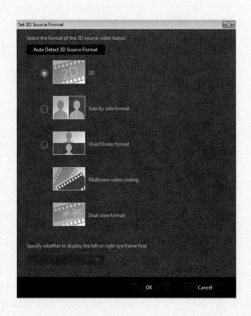

On the option panel that opens, select the 2D or 3D format of your video – or simply click the **Auto Detect** button at the top of the panel.

We discuss 3D video editing in detail beginning on page 81.

Manually set up your project

In most cases, you'll not need to configure your project's settings. You'll simply set the **Aspect Ratio** (see page 42), import your media and go to work.

However, there are times (such as when you want your project to have a particular frame rate or you want **5.1 Surround** rather than **Stereo** audio (see page 224) when you'll want to configure your project's settings manually.

To access the project set-up screen, click the **Cog** at the top of the program and then select the **General** page.

On this preference page, you can set your project's frame rate to **24 frames per second** (which will give your movie a more filmic look), standard PAL **25** or standard NTSC **30** fps, or PAL **50** or NTSC **60** fps. The faster your frame rate, the smoother the action and movement in your videos will look.

Don't worry too much about the **Drop Frame** option. Leave it set to **Yes**. This setting compensates for the fact that NTSC video is actually 29.97 frames per second, and "dropping frames" allows the program to treat the video as if it's actually 30 fps.)

Although the old **25 fps/30 fps** standards are still most common, more and more videomakers are choosing to create videos at **24, 50** or **60** fps – particularly as most HDTVs are now capable of playing at the higher frame rates. If you add media to your project that is at a different frame rate than the frame rate you've set up in these preferences, the program will blend the frames to match your project's frame rate. The program can edit video with frame rates as high as 240 frames per second!

The **Editing** preference page includes some additional project settings worth exploring, including settings for the default length for still photos or titles you add to your project.

The video and audio formats and video resolutions that are available for you to output are ultimately determined by your project settings. For a list of available output options based on your project settings, see page 196.

Prepping Video in the Media Room

Adding, Trimming and Splitting Clips

Powerful Tools Available Through the Function Buttons

The Video Speed Designer

The Video Collage Designer

Working in 3D

360° Video Editing

Blending Effects

Chapter 6

Edit on the Timeline

Turning clips into movies

The Timeline is where your media files become a movie.

It's where you remove what you don't want, enhance what you do and arrange the whole thing into something that tells a story.

Once you've gathered your media files into your project, as described in **Chapter 5,** they become the library of assets – video, still photos, music and other audio – that you will use to tell your story.

This library of assets resides in a panel that CyberLink calls the **Media Room**, opened by clicking the tab along the upper left of the program.

A **Search the Library** box in the upper right of the **Room** allows you to real-time search for a specific file.

Media Room views

There are a number of ways to view your media files in the **Media Room**. Some of these views make your media files easier to identify, while others make more efficient use of the panel's space or allow you to sort or filter your media files to make it easier to find a specific clip.

Filter your media views

To display only the video, audio or still images in your project, or any combination, toggle the media filters at the top center of the **Media Room**.

Sort your media files

To change the order that your media files are displayed, click the **Library Menu** button at the top of **Media Room**.

A drop down menu will appear. Select the **Sort** sub-menu and you will find options to arrange your media files by **Name, Duration, File Size, Date** or **Type**.

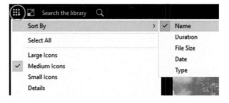

Change how your media files are displayed

To change how your media files are displayed in this panel, click the **Library Menu** at the top of the **Media Room** and set whether your media is displayed as **Large Icons, Medium Icons, Small Icons** or **Details** (a list of clip names and properties).

You can also control the size of the icons precisely by clicking the **Adjust Thumbnail Size** button just right of the **Library Menu** button.

Additional Media Room options

In addition to the media you import into your PowerDirector project, the **Media Room** includes access to additional video and sound files. To access this content, select from the categories on the left side of the panel.

Media Content, the default setting, displays your main media library, consisting of the video, still photos, music and other audio files you've added to your project.

Color Boards gives you access to a library of color panels that can be used for backgrounds, foregrounds and other forms of media in your project.

To create a custom color for this library, click the **Create a New Color Board** button at the top center of the **Color Boards** panel.

Color Boards

Create a New Color Board

Background Music displays a library of 50 free royalty-free musical clips in a variety of styles, all of which you can used without restriction in your video projects. Once a clip is downloaded, it becomes a permanent part of your music library and it can be added directly to your timeline from this panel. (Additionally royalty-free music can be purchased from the **Audio Network**.)

Background Music

Sound Clips displays a library of 100 sound effects, including everything from background sounds to animals to explosions to fist fights. As with **Background Music**, once you've downloaded one of these sound effects, it becomes a permanent part of your sound library.

Sound Clips

57

Project Room media

In some ways an extension of the **Media Room**, the **Project Room** includes additional material from which to build your projects.

>   **My Projects** displays your CyberLink PowerDirector projects as thumbnails. As we discuss on page 65, PowerDirector projects can be embedded – used as is as media files in other projects.

My Projects

>   **Express Projects** are templates, including titles and effects, that you can use to semi-automatically build your video projects. For information on using **Express Project** templates, see **Chapter 4**.

Content Aware Editing

The PowerDirector **Media Room** tool can analyze your video clips

Express Projects

for quality issues. To use this tool, **right-click** on a clip in the **Media Room** and select **Edit Using Content Aware Editing**.

The program will analyze your clip and indicate segments of the clip that include **Zooms, Pans, Faces, Speech, Motion, Shaky Video** and **Poor Lighting**.

Based on those characteristics, you then have the option of trimming the clip into one or several shorter clips, as discussed in the sidebar on the facing page.

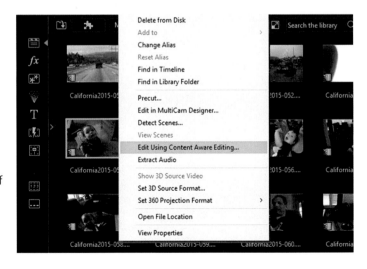

Trim a longer clip with Content Aware Editing

Often you have a longer clip but you only want to use a short segment – or a couple of segments – from it in your movie. (A similar, if somewhat simplified version of this workspace is found in the **Trim** tool, discussed on page 67.)

You may also want to trim around poor quality segments of this clip, as indicated by the **Content Aware Editing** panel, discussed on the facing page.

To open the **Content Aware Editing** trimmer, **right-click** on the clip in the **Media Room** and select **Edit Using Content Aware Editing**. Once the program completes its analysis, a **Timeline** along the bottom of the **Content Aware Editing** panel will indicate content and quality issues in your clip.

To create a shorter segment of your clip, position this **Timeline's** playhead where you'd like your segment to begin and click **Mark In**, as illustrated below. Then position the playhead where you'd like the segment to end and click **Mark Out**. You can adjust the length of this segment by dragging the **In** and **Out** points on this **Timeline**.

Click the **Selected** button. A segment will be created and the tool will offer to automatically fix your quality issues. Your saved segments will be listed on the right side of the panel.

Create as many segments as you'd like.

When you click **OK**, these selected segments will be added to your project's timeline at the position of the playhead.

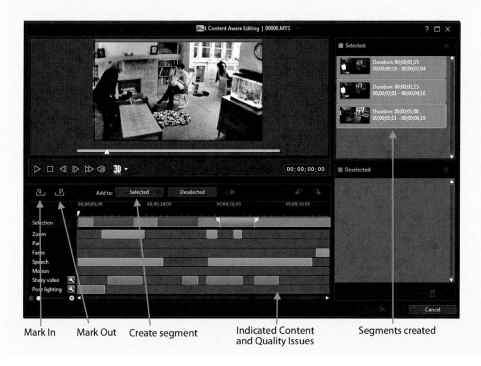

Mark In   Mark Out   Create segment   Indicated Content and Quality Issues   Segments created

Break a clip into scenes

Once you've added a clip to your **Media Room** library, the program can break it into shorter scenes, based on the clip's content.

To break a clip into scenes, **right-click** on the clip in the **Media Room** and select **Detect Scenes...**

The program will analyze the clip and break it into scenes, placing these trimmed clips inside a sub-folder linked to the main media clip.

Right-click and select Detect Scenes.
The program will split up the clip, based on content.

Edit in MultiCam Designer...
Detect Scenes...
View Scenes
Edit Using Content Aware Editing...
Extract Audio

The scenes will appear in a sub-folder in the Media Room.

To view scenes sub-folder from the main Media Room directory, click on the folder icon on the main clip icon.

Bird.m2ts

Add media clips to the Timeline

Adding video and audio clips to your timeline is pretty much as simple as dragging the clips from the **Media Room** to a track on the **Timeline**.

However, when you insert a clip into an assemblage of clips on your timeline or over an existing clip, the program will prompt you with a number of options.

Overwrite — Ctrl+Drop
Trim to Fit
Speed up to Fit
Insert
Insert and Move All Clips — Shift+Drop
Crossfade — Alt+Drop

Depending on how many clips your new clip will overlay or if you are placing your clips between existing clips, PowerDirector may ask you if you would like to:

Overwrite the existing clips on your timeline.

Trim to Fit, if you're placing the clip in an empty spot between two clips.

Speed up to Fit, if you're placing the clip in an empty spot between clips.

Insert to ripple the clips on this video/audio track only to the right.

Insert and Move All clips to ripple the clips on *all* video and audio tracks on your timeline to the right.

Crossfade, or fill the gap and add a crossfade to the clips it will overlay.

Video 1, at the top of the **Timeline,** is the main video track. It will also be the *bottom* video track as you build your movie. In other words, the video text and effects you add on **Video tracks 2, 3,** etc. will appear over the video on **Video 1** in your movie, despite being under it on the **Timeline** itself. (If you'd prefer, however, the **Timeline** track view listing can be reversed, as we show you on page 12.)

You can add up to 100 video and audio tracks to the **Timeline.** For more information on the managing and viewing the timeline, see **The Timeline** on page 10.

Trim a clip on your timeline

Trimming a clip means removing video or audio from the clip's beginning or end.

The most common way to trim a clip on your timeline is to click to select the clip, then hover your mouse over the end of a clip until the **Trim** indicator appears, as in the illustration on the facing page. Click and drag left or right to remove footage or extend the clip. (You can get more precise trims if you zoom into your timeline.)

When you **Trim** a clip, a pop-up menu will ask if you'd like to:

> **Trim Only,** which trims the clips but keeps the rest of your timeline in place, leaving a gap at the point of your trim.
>
> **Trim and Move Clips,** which moves only clips on that video/audio track left to fill in the gap.
>
> **Trim and Move All Clips** ripples all tracks left to fill in the gap.

As an alternative, you can select a clip on your timeline and click the **Trim** button (the scissors icon) along the top left of the **Timeline.** This will open the **Trim** tool in which you can set in and out points for your clip.

For a detailed discussion of the **Trim** tool, see page 67.

Split clips to slice through your clips at the position of the playhead.

Split a clip on your timeline

Splitting a clip on your timeline means slicing it into two or more pieces so that you can delete a portion of the clip or so that you can apply an effect or an adjustment to only a segment of the clip.

Splitting a clip is as simple as positioning the playhead where you'd like the split to appear and then clicking the **Timeline's Split** button.

> **If you have several tracks of clips** and you have *no clips selected* on your timeline, your split will slice through *every clip* on every track.
>
> **If you have a clip selected on your timeline**, only that clip will be split.

Delete clips from your timeline

To delete a clip from your timeline, select it and press the **Delete** button on your keyboard. The program will ask you if you want to:

> **Remove and Leave Gap**, in which the clip will be removed and no other clips will move, leaving a gap on your timeline.
>
> **Remove and Fill Gap**, which ripples the clips on this video/audio track only left to fill the gap.
>
> **Remove, Fill Gap and Move All Clips**, which ripples the clips on all tracks left to fill the gap.

As an alternative, you can skip this pop-up menu and use keyboard combinations to remove your clip in a single move.

> **Shift+Delete** will remove the clip and leave a gap on your timeline.
>
> **Ctrl+Delete** will remove the clip and ripple the clips left to fill in the gap on this track only.
>
> **Alt+Delete** will remove the clip and ripple the clips on all tracks.

Select, copy and paste clips

To select several clips on your timeline, hold down the **Shift** or **Ctrl** key as you select your clips. You can also select a number of clips by clicking and dragging from a spot on the **Timeline** that has no clips over the clips you want to select.

To **Cut** from your timeline, select a clip or clips and **right-click** or select the **Cut** option from the **Edit** menu. The program will offer three options:

Cut and Leave Gap, in which the clip will be removed and no other clips will move, leaving a gap on your timeline.

Cut and Fill Gap, which ripples the clips on only this video/audio track left to fill the gap.

Cut, Fill Gap and Move All Clips, which ripples the clips on all tracks left to fill the gap.

To **Copy** a clip or clips on your timeline, **right-click** or select **Cut** from the **Edit** menu – or use the Windows shortcut **Ctrl+c**. Because copying doesn't affect your timeline, you will see no pop-up options menu.

To **Paste** a clip or clips to your timeline, select the video/audio track on which you'd like the clip to be pasted and position the playhead where you'd like this paste to begin, then **right-click** or select the **Paste** option from the **Edit** menu – or use the Windows shortcut **Ctrl+v.**

If you have the playhead positioned on your timeline at a point where the pasted clip(s) will not fill a gap and will not overlay existing clips, the **Ctrl+v** shortcut simply pastes to the timeline with no pop-up menu options.

If your paste will place your clips into a gap between clips or onto an existing clip on your timeline, the program will offer you a number of options:

Paste and Overwrite the existing clips.

Paste and Trim to Fit, if you're placing the clip in a gap between two clips.

Paste and Speed up to Fit, if you're placing the clip in a gap between clips.

Paste and Insert to ripple the clips on this video/audio track only.

Paste, Insert and Move All Clips to ripple the clips on all tracks on your timeline.

Crossfade, fill the gap and add a crossfade to the clip(s) it will overlay.

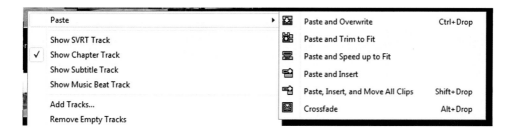

Add a Fade In or Fade Out

There are a number of ways to add a Fade In or a Fade Out to a video clip on your timeline:

A **Fade In** or **Fade Out** can be added to a clip by opening it in the **Designer/PiP Designer** panel and checking the option, as illustrated on page 69.

A **Fade In** and a **Fade Out** can be added simultaneously to a clip on your timeline by **right-clicking** on the clip and, from the **Edit Video** sub-menu, selecting **Enable Fade In and Fade Out**.

When a Fade option is selected in the PiP Designer, Opacity keyframes are added to the clip's timeline.

An audio or video **Fade In** or **Fade Out** can manually be added to a clip on your timeline by keyframing the clip's audio level or video opacity. To add a keyframe hold down the **Ctrl** key as you click on the horizontal green

Keyframes can also be added to a clip's Opacity or Audio Level directly on the timeline or via the right-click menu.

Opacity line or the blue **Audio Level** line running through the clip. Once added, a keyframe can be raised or lowered to increase or decrease a level. A ramp from a zero % level keyframe to a 100% level keyframe will create a **Fade In**. (More information on keyframe audio levels can be found in **Setting audio levels with Keyframe Settings** on page 137.)

An important thing to note about video **Fade Ins** and **Fade Outs** is that they are the result of a transition of **Opacity** (the opposite of transparency). So, when you are at zero **Opacity**, you will only see a black screen when the clip is on **Video 1** – because there is nothing on a video track below it. However, if your clip is on an *upper* video track, 0% **Opacity** (or 100% transparency) will *show the video on the track below it* – and your fade in will actually appear as a dissolve from the lower video clip to the upper.

Remove audio or video from a clip

To remove the audio or video from a clip on your timeline, **right-click** on it and select **Unlink Audio and Video**. Once the audio and video for the clip are unlinked, you can select either its video or its audio and remove it by pressing the **Delete** key on your keyboard.

If you'd prefer, you can also simply disable to the audio on a clip by **right-clicking** on it and selecting **Mute Clip**.

Use a movie project as media in another project

One of the most advanced features in
PowerDirector Ultimate is its ability to
embed a project within another project.

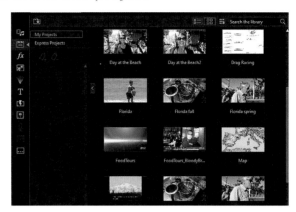

In other words an project-in-the-works,
without being rendered, can be used as
if it were a single media clip in another
project – a feature usually only seen
in professional video editing apps.
In this way you can work on a longer
video project in short pieces and then
combine each of these segments into a
master project mix.

To access your project files, go to the
Project Room and select the **My Projects** category. The panel will display
the PowerDirector projects on your hard drive.

Drag a project to your timeline or storyboard as if it were a media clip. The
project will appear as a single media clip on your timeline.

In the upper left of the **Timeline**, the current project will appear as a tab.
Any projects you have added to your timeline will appear as additional
tabs.

If you click on your embedded project's tab, the project will appear on
your timeline, where you can edit it in real time. (Do note, however, that if
you edit your embedded project and change its duration, you may need to
tweak its placement on your main timeline.)

Once a project has been added as media to a timeline, it can be further edited by selecting its timeline tab.

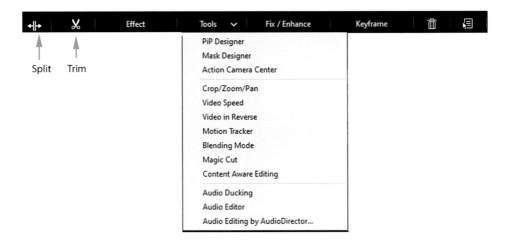

Function Buttons

When you select a clip on your timeline, **Function Buttons** will appear along the top of the **Timeline**. Which buttons appear depends on the nature of your clip and if an effect has been added to it:

Split slices your clips, as discussed on page 62.

Trim (the scissors button) opens a panel for precisely trimming your clip, as described in **Trim or Precut a clip** on page 67.

Effect (visible only if you have an effect applied to your selected clip) opens the clip's **Effects Settings**, in which you can customize your effect (see page 106).

Tools includes options for opening the **PiP Designer** (see page 69), or the **Mask Designer** (see page 123), a workspace for using shapes and text as "cookie cutters" to create custom shapes for your video, as well as the **Action Camera Center** (page 114), a workspace for cleaning up and adding speed effects to your action camera video.

If you are working with 360° video, the **View Designer** (see page 83) can be used to control how this video is displayed. You'll also find links here to the **Crop/Zoom/Pan** tool (see page 127), **Action Camera Center** (page 114), **Video Speed Designer** (see page 72), **Video in Reverse** option, **Motion Tracker** (page 112), **Blending Mode** controller (see page 84), **Magic Cut** moviemaking wizard (see **Chapter 13**) and **Content Aware Editing** (see page 58).

If your clip is or includes audio, you will find options for setting **Audio Ducking**, opening your clip in the built-in **Audio Editor** or opening your clip in the external **AudioDirector** program, if you have it installed.

Fix/Enhance (page 70) opens a panel for adjusting your clip's lighting, color and audio.

Keyframe (page 126) opens a panel in which you can create animations or make adjustments and customize effects and have their levels or positions change over time.

Trim or Precut a clip

The **Trim** tool is a sophisticated workspace for selecting one or more video segments from a longer video clip on your timeline.

A similar workspace, the **Precut** tool, can be used to selected one or more video segments from a longer clip that is still in your **Media Room**.

To pre-trim a clip in the Media Room, right-click and select Precut...

Segments that are selected with the **Trim** tool are added to your timeline. Segments that are selected with the **Precut** tool are saved to a sub-folder in your **Media Room**.

However, the look and functions of the **Precut** and the **Trim** workspaces are otherwise identical.

To trim segments from a clip a clip on the Timeline, click the scissors button.

Precut a clip in the Media Room

1 **Open a clip the Precut panel**

   Right-click on a clip in the **Media Room** and select **Precut...** The **Precut** tool will open, as illustrated on page 68.

   Create your sub-clip(s), as described in **Select a segment or segments from your clip** on page 68.

2 **Save your sub-clips**

   Click **OK**. Your selected segments will be saved to a sub-folder in the **Media Room**, accessible by clicking the folder icon that appears in the lower right of the master clip.

Trim a clip on the Timeline

1 **Open the Trim panel**

   With your clip selected on your project timeline, click the **Trim** button (scissors) on the upper left of the **Timeline**. The **Trim** tool will open, as illustrated on page 68.

   Create your sub-clip(s), as described in **Select a segment or segments from your clip** as discussed on page 68.

2 **Save your selected clips to your timeline**

   Click **OK**. Your selected segment(s) will replace the clip on the **Timeline**.

Select a segment from your clip

To select a **single segment** from your clip:

1   **Set an in point**

    Click on the **Single Trim** tab on the upper left of the panel. Play your clip and pause it or drag the playhead to the point in your clip you'd like your selected segment to begin.

To creat a Single Trim, set In and Out points on the Timeline.

    Click the **Mark In** button or press open brackets [on your keyboard. Your **In Position** will appear as a thumbnail on the right side of the panel.

2   **Set an out point**

    Reposition the playhead to the end of the segment you want to select and click the **Mark Out** button or press close brackets] on your keyboard. Your **Out Position** will appear as a thumbnail on the right side of the panel.

Your segment's in and out point markers can also be simply dragged into position on the **Timeline**.

Select multiple clips from a longer clip

To select **multiple segments** from your clip:

1   **Set an in point**

    Click on the **Multi Trim** tab on the upper left of the panel. Play your clip and pause it or drag the playhead to the point in your clip you'd like your selected segment to begin. Click the **Mark In** button or press open brackets [on your keyboard.

Timeline zoom resizer   Scene Detection based on content

To create Multi Trim segments, set several In and Out points on the Timeline.

2   **Set an out point**

Reposition the playhead to the end of the segment you want to select and click the **Mark Out** button or press close brackets] on your keyboard.

Your segment will appear as a **Selected Segment** on the right side of the panel.

As you continue to add in and out point markers, new **Selected Segments** will be added to this list.

As an alternative to manually making selections, you can click the **Scene Detection** button. Segments will be selected automatically based on changes in your clip's content.

The PiP Designer

When you **double-click** a clip on your timeline or when you click on a clip and then select the **PiP Designer** option under the **Tools** Function Button, the **PiP Designer** will open.

Many of the features in this panel are designed for creating effects when using your video clip on an upper video track. We discuss a number of these features in more detail in **Chapter 11, PiP and Multitrack Video Effects**. And we show you how to use the powerful **Chroma Key** effect on page 109 of **Chapter 9, Video Effects and Animations**.

The **PiP Designer** is also where you can add **Fade Ins** and **Fade Outs** to your clips, as illustrated below.

Fade Ins and Fade Outs create Opacity keyframes.

Fix/Enhance tools

When you select a clip on your timeline and click the **Fix/Enhance** Function Button along the top of the **Timeline**, the **Fix/Enhance** panel opens.

In this panel, you can check and select a number of picture adjusters and set the levels for each using a slider.

We discuss this panel's entire set of **Color Enhancement** tools in detail beginning on page 100 of **Chapter 9, Video Effects and Animations**.

Additionally, you'll find a number of these **Fix/Enhance tools** included in the **Action Camera Center**, as discussed on page 114.

White Balance

One of my favorite tools, the **White Balance** tool, will can be used to correct color temperature/tint issues in your video clips. Levels of **Temperature** and **Tint** can be set manually – or, you can click on the **Sampler** (the eye dropper) under **White Calibration** and click to indicate a white spot in your video. The tool will set the clip's white balance automatically!

To adjust your White Balance, manually adjust the Color Temperature and Tint...

... or select the eye dropper and use it to sample a white spot in the White Calibration panel.

Correct lens distortion

Sometimes, when you've shot video with an action camera or you've used an extremely wide angle lens on your camcorder, your video can take on a "fish eye" distortion, with some unwanted rounding of the image.

When you select the **Lens Correction** Fix/Enhance option, the panel will open a set of simple tools for correcting this distortion.

Camera lens correction presets

Often adjusting the **Fish-eye Distortion** slider alone will correct the problem. But, if you need it, the **Vignette Amount** slider will also smooth out any uneven lighting.

Also worth checking out at the top of the panel is a drop-down library of presets, giving you the ability to automatically correct your lens distortion and vignetting issues simply by selecting the brand and model of your camera from the lists!

Additional tools for correcting and enhancing your action camera footage can be found in the **Action Camera Center**, as discussed on page 114.

Stabilize your shaky video

Often your handheld videos have a bit more shake in them than you'd prefer. Handheld and shaky movies draw attention to the camera, which is probably not something you want (unless you're shooting a horror film and the camera represents the killer's point of view). Fortunately, PowerDirector comes with a very effective – and pretty much automatic – tool for stabilizing your video.

To stabilize your video, select the clip on your timeline that you want to take the shake out of, click the **Fix/Enhance** Function Button, then check the **Video Stabilizer** option on the **Fix/Enhance** panel.

The default settings usually do a great job, but we recommend, for best results, adjusting the slider so that you're using the *minimal* amount of stabilizing to get the job done. (The higher the setting, the more the **Stabilizer** reduces your video's resolution.)

But be careful: The more stabilization is applied, the more negative impact the tool will have on the clarity and quality of your finished movie.

The Video Speed Designer

Relatively new to PowerDirector is a cool workspace for controlling the playback speed of your video at precise points. With the **Video Speed Designer**, you can not only control how fast or how slow your video plays, but you can also set your video clip's playback to shift from fast or slow to normal speed at precise points in the clip. In fact, you can create several **Time Shift** ranges in a single clip and have it change playback speed any number of times.

To open the **Video Speed Designer**, select a clip on your timeline and then click the **Tools** Function Button along the top of the timeline and select the **Video Speed** option.

In the **Video Speed Designer**, you can set the playback speed of the **Entire Clip** or for a **Selected Range** (or ranges). Just select the tab for the adjustment you want to make.

Change the speed of your Entire Clip

If you are setting the playback speed for your **Entire Clip**, set your speed by either changing the **New Video Duration** or **Speed Multiplier**. Either option can be set using the adjusters or by simply overwriting the number that represents its setting.

Changing one setting automatically changes the other. In other words, if you change your **New Video Duration** to half its original length, the **Speed Multiplier** will automatically shift to 2x.

Change the speed of a Selected Range

In the **Video Speed Designer**, you also have the option of selecting one or more segments or **Ranges** on your clip and then applying a speed change or **Time Shift** to that segment. Each **Range** can have its own separate **Time Shift** settings applied to it.

continued on next page

With a clip selected on your timeline, select Power Tools from the Tools menu, then click the Speed Adjustment button under Video Speed settings.

In the Video Speed Designer, apply a Duration or Speed Multiplier to your entire clip or to selected Time Shift ranges, created by positioning the playhead and click the Create Time Shift button.

To create a **Range**, position the playhead where you'd like the **Range** to begin and then click one of the **Create Time Shift** buttons. Both the **Create Time Shift** button on the timeline and the button on the settings panel do the same thing: Create a one second **Range** on your timeline, indicated by a yellow-orange overlay.

By dragging the handles on either end of this **Range**, you can change its length or its location on your clip.

You may create as many **Ranges** as you'd like on a clip. The currently selected **Range** – the one you will be applying your settings to – will be yellow-orange. Unselected **Ranges** will appear as blue.

With a **Range** selected, change either the **Duration** of the segment or set the **Speed Multiplier**. As when you set the speed for your **Entire Clip**, changing one setting automatically changes the other. In other words, changing the **Speed Multiplier** to 2x automatically changes the **Duration** to half of the **Range's** original length.

The **Ease In** and **Ease Out** options are simple interpolations for controlling how abruptly your video goes into and out of its **Time Shifts**. Easing in or out of a **Time Shift**, for instance, ramps up or slows down your video rather abruptly shifting its speed to fast or slow motion.

Remove a **Range** by selecting it on the timeline and clicking on the **Trash Can** icon.

By default, your audio will match the playback speed of your video – which can sometimes produce an unwanted effect. You may or may not want your audio slowing to a crawl as your video slips into slow motion.

Clicking on the **Cog** (preferences) on the upper right of the timeline gives you access to options for controlling the pitch of the audio so that its change in speed isn't quite so jarring as well as the option to remove the audio completely from your time-shifted clip. (Note that the pitch control is really only effective between .5x and 2x playback speed.)

Another option available under **Video Speed Designer** settings is to **Apply Interpolated Technology When Available**. **Interpolated Technology** blends frames for video that has had a slow motion effect applied to it, and the result can be a much cleaner, smoother slo-mo sequence.

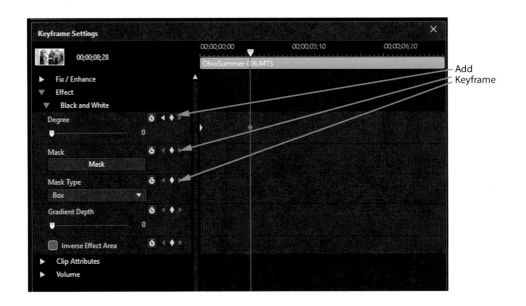

The Keyframe workspace

Keyframing is a function in which levels of an effect or properties like scale, position and opacity can be set to vary over time. Keyframes can be used to create animations or effects that transition over time.

When you select a clip on your timeline and click the **Keyframe** Function Button along the top of the **Timeline**, the **Keyframe Settings** panel will open. The panel will display a list of your clip's properties, many of which can be adjusted by clicking on the corresponding **Function Button**. They are:

> **Fix/Enhance** (as described on page 70), which includes **Lighting, Video Denoise, Audio Denoise, Video Enhancement, Color Adjustment** and **White Balance**.
>
> **Effects,** if any have been added to your clip, as discussed in **Chapter 9**.
>
> **Clip Attributes** (adjusted in the **Modify/Pip Designer**, as described on page 69), including **Opacity, Scale, Rotation, Position/Motion** and **2D to 3D** levels.
>
> **Volume** level (if your clip includes audio).

The **Keyframe Settings** panel is a workspace for creating animations and transitions with any of these properties. To add a keyframe, click the **Add Keyframe** button next to a setting. A diamond-shaped keyframe representing setting will be created.

As illustrated above, every property is displayed with a timeline representing the duration of your clip. At the head of each timeline is a yellow diamond, a keyframe representing a setting for this property. To add a second keyframe, move the playhead on this timeline and change a property or effect's setting. A new keyframe representing that setting will automatically be created.

The program will create the animation or transition between these two keyframes. In the illustration above, for instance, the **Degree** of the **Black and White** effect will begin at 200 and, at the second keyframe, will drop to zero. The result will be a transition of the clip from black and white to color.

Storyboard Mode

Most often you'll likely be editing on the traditional **Timeline**. It allows you to layer video and add titles and effects on upper video tracks. However, the program also offers a simplified **Storyboard Mode** for quickly assembling your movie.

To toggle between **Storyboard Mode** and **Timeline Mode**, select either mode from the program's **View** menu or press the **Tab** button on your keyboard.

In **Storyboard View**, only one video/audio track is available, and the clips are simply dragged to fill placeholders. The order of your clips can be re-arranged by dragging the clip thumbnails around and between the other clips.

The **Function Buttons** along the top of the **Storyboard Timeline** function the same way as they do in **Timeline Mode** (see page 66), and you can switch back and forth between **Timeline Mode** and **Storyboard Mode** at any time as you edit your movie.

We discuss keyframing in more detail on page 126 of **Chapter 9, Video Effects and Fixes**.

Drag Region markers left or right to define a Timeline Region.

Select and output a Range of your timeline

When you define a **Range** on your timeline (by spreading the yellow tabs on either side of the playhead), you indicate a segment of your timeline for a specific use.

If you **right-click** on your selected **Range**, you will find options setting this area to play it as a **Loop** continuously (so you can focus on it) or to **Produce** it (output a video of this defined area of your movie rather than your entire movie).

Right-click options for your selected Timeline Range.

When a frame is selected, the clip's editing tools become activated.

Open the Video Collage Designer.

Select a Layout template.

Drag video clips into the template.

Create a split screen effect with the Video Collage Designer

PowerDirector includes a relatively new tool for creating cool-looking split screen video collages. These collages can include up to seven videos running simultaneously (although you may find your computer bogging down a bit after three or four). Best of all, it makes creating this rather complicated effect very simple and intuitive.

To create a **Video Collage**:

1   **Open the Video Collage Designer**

Select **Video Collage Designer** from the **Plugins** menu at the top of the program.

2   **Select a Collage Layout**

From the top of the panel, choose the **Layout** template for your collage. The collage template will appear in the preview window.

3   **Add video to your layout.**

Drag video clips from the media thumbnail listing on the left into your template. Additional clips by can added from your hard drive by clicking the **Import Media** button.

4   **Customize your video clip's properties.**

A timecode will appear over each video clip indicating the clip's running time.

If you click on a clip in the collage, editing tools will become activated, as illustrated to the right.

> The **slider** will enlarge or shrink the size of your video within the template. (If you click and drag on the video, you can also adjust the video's position within the template grid.)
>
> The **audio toggle** sets whether the video clip's audio plays as the video clip plays or its audio is muted.
>
> Clicking the **scissors** icon opens your video in a simplified trimming workspace in which you can set your clip's start and end points.

In the next step, you'll set whether the clips in your collage play one after another or all at once. If your clips are all playing at once, you may want to trim them so that they are all the same duration. If your clips are of different duration, the shorter clips will freeze after playback until the longer clips complete their playback – an effect you probably don't want.

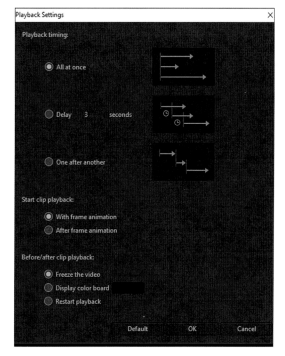

5   **Select your collage's settings.**

When you click the **Settings** button to the right of the preview window, you'll find options to set whether the clips in your collage play one after another or all at once. If you select the **All At Once** option, you can also select how the shorter clips display while the longer clips are playing.

The **Playback Settings** panel also includes the option the begin or end your collage with an animation.

6   **Save your collage**

Once you click **OK**, you'll be returned to the editing workspace and your collage will appear on your timeline with a "collage" indicator on the left side of the clip.

To re-open the **Video Collage Designer** and re-edit your collage, select the clip on your timeline and click the **Video Collage** Function Button that appears along the top of the **Timeline**.

Edit 3D video

CyberLink includes a wealth of tools for working with 3D video and even creating 3D content.

Creating a 3D video project is easy. Just add your 3D video and PowerDirector will auto-detect your 3D content and offer to adjust your project settings accordingly.

3DTrain.AVI

3D clips are identified by a little "**3D**" in the upper left corner.

Among the unique features in PowerDirector is an amazing tool for creating a rather effective 3D-looking video from standard 2D video. We show you how to use it in the sidebar on the facing page.

The program also includes a number of output options for your finished 3D video.

Set your 3D Source Format

In most cases, PowerDirector will auto-detect your 3D footage and set up your project accordingly. However, because 3D video comes in a variety of source formats, you may need to designate the clip's format.

To do so, **right-click** on the clip in your **Media Room** library and select **Set 3D Source Format**. Then select from the following options:

> **2D** advises the program that your clip is actually a 2D video.

> **Side by Side Format**, if your 3D video uses a format which has the right and left images side-by-side, PowerDirector will merge them together to create the 3D image.

> **Multiview Video Coding** if your 3D video is of the high-def MVC format.

> **Dual View Format** if your video uses the dual view AVI format.

Preview window settings for your 3D footage

The **Preview** window includes a number of ways to view your 3D video files. To access them, click the **3D** icon to the right of the playback controls.

When you select **Auto Detect**, your 3D video will usually display as **anaglyphic**.

Anaglyph video displays the right and left channels of your stereoscopic 3D video as shades of red and cyan. The chief advantage to viewing your video in **Anaglyph Red/Cyan** is that you don't need any special equipment

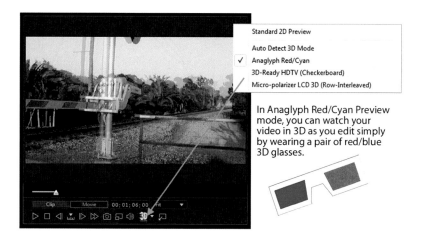

In Anaglyph Red/Cyan Preview mode, you can watch your video in 3D as you edit simply by wearing a pair of red/blue 3D glasses.

to view the 3D image – except for a pair of standard red/blue 3D glasses. This makes it very simple for you to check the effectiveness of your 3D as you work on any computer system.

The other 3D preview options are **3D-Ready HDTV** and **Micropolarizer LCD 3D**, which may require specialized equipment to view effectively.

2D to 3D

One of the most amazing tools in PowerDirector is a tool which creates faux 3D content from standard 3D video – and the results are strikingly effective!

To create 3D video from your video, select the video clip on your timeline and click the **More Features** Function Button along the top of the Timeline.

On the context menu that opens, click S**elect Clip Attributes/Convert 2D to 3D**. On the panel that opens, check **Turn on 2D to 3D Conversion**. Click the **Apply to All** button to apply **2D to 3D** to all clips on your timeline.

If you'd prefer, you can also set the 3D display to be displayed as **Standard 2D Preview** so that you can focus on editing rather than the 3D.

Your Preview settings do not affect the format or look of your final video output.

Output your 3D video

Editing your 3D video isn't all that much different than editing regular 3D video. And PowerDirector includes a number of great options for outputting your finished piece.

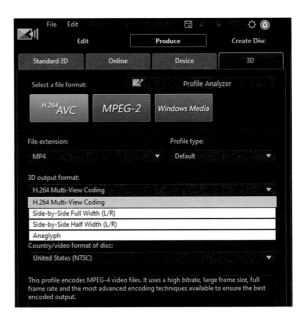

Click the **Produce** button at the top of the interface then, in the **Produce** workspace, click on the **3D** tab.

Select an output format.

Windows Media produces a WMV file. This format includes profiles for 320x180, 640x360, 1280x720 and 1920x1080.

MPEG-2. A format that includes profiles for outputting DVD-ready 720x480, 720x576, 1280x720, 1440x1080 and BluRay-ready 1920x1080.

AVC. An H.264 compressed format that can be used to output an MP4, M2TS or MKV file. These various file formats include profiles for outputting 640x480, 720x480, 720x576, 1280x720, 1440x1080 and 1920x1080 video at a variety of frame rates. MP4s and M2TSs also include the option to output the 3D video in the **MVC (Multi-View Coding)** format.

Additionally, you have the option of creating custom profiles for any format.

All 3D output templates give you the option of outputting **Side-by-Side (L/R)** or **Anaglyph** 3D. **Anaglyph** 3D can be viewed on any device with a pair of red/blue 3D glasses. **Side-by-Side** 3D requires a monitor or TV capable of displaying it.

MVC, or Multi-view Video Coding, is an advanced 3D video encoder that saves visual data from several cameras as a single video stream. **3D BluRay discs use the MVC coded video.** MVC is also backwards compatible, so that it can be viewed as 3D on a 3D enabled device or 2D when played on a standard TV.

BluRay discs can also be output in the **3D-BD** format. For information creating 3D DVDs and BluRay discs, see page 217.

Edit 360° video

PowerDirector 19 includes a powerful workspace for editing **360° video**.

360° video is usually shot with a globe-shaped or square camcorder that records not just what the camcorder is pointed at but up to a complete circle or globe around the camcorder.

360 editing can be done with the Preview Window set to 360 or standard mode.

The resultant video can be displayed on a computer, YouTube or Facebook or viewed through inexpensive VR goggles and, as the video is playing, the viewer can choose what he or she looks at.

A PowerDirector 360° project can be made up of 360° video or from still photos patched together using a freely available app for your smartphone. You can even use standard video in a 360° project and the program will turn it into 360-like video.

Create a 360° project

Creating a 360° video is as simple as selecting the **360°** option from the **Aspect Ratio** drop-down menu at the top of the program. To see the video in its 360° view, click the **360°** button on the **Preview Window**.

Optionally, your video can also be displayed in the **Preview Window** in standard view (as illustrated above), in which case the entire 360° image will preview as flattened. This is probably how you'll view the video as you're doing your basic editing.

When your **Preview Window** is set to 360° view (indicated by the 360° marker in the upper left corner, seen in the illustration above), you'll be able to navigate the video, just as your viewer will, by simply dragging over the image.

Full 360° video can be navigated in pretty much any direction – left and right and up and down. A sample of 360° video (called **Beach 360.mp4**) is included with the program. As you can see if you load it to the timeline and play it in 360° view, as the video plays, you can decide which direction you want to look – as if you are inside a ball and the video completely surrounds you!

Use non-360° imagery

If you add non-360° video to a project set up for the **360° Aspect Ratio** the program will create faux 360° video for it. (Although it may also warn you that you're using video that is the wrong aspect ratio for your project.)

When you add, say, standard 16:9 video to a 360° project, the program will essentially wrap the video completely around the viewer. The resultant video captures some of the magic of 360° – but, particularly if you're using a lot of close-ups in the video, it can also look rather odd and distorted.

If you don't have a 360° camcorder, there are many "panorama camera" apps available for your smartphone that will guide you through the process of taking photos and stitching them together to form a 360° still image. These "pano" photos can be quite effective in a 360° project!

Output your 360° video

Naturally, in order for your viewers to see your video in all its 360° glory, you'll need to output it in a format or to a site that supports the 360° navigation.

If your project is set up for the **360° Aspect Ratio**, only 360° output options will be available when you click the **Produce** tab at the top of the program. (360° is not supported on DVDs or BluRay discs.)

The **360° Video** tab in the **Produce** includes the option to output your video as either an H.264 (AVC) or H.265 (HEVC) MP4. A 360° MP4 can be output at 1280x640, 1920x960, 2560x1280, 2880x1440, 3840x1920 and 4096x2048 resolutions at 24 or 30 frames per second.

Under the **Online** tab, you'll find options for uploading directly to **YouTube** and **Vimeo**, both of which support 360° navigation. Your videos' can be given titles, descriptions and keyword tags, and your **YouTube** upload can posted to a selected category.

Use 360° video in a standard project

Just as you may occasionally want to use standard video or photos in a 360° project, you may occasionally want to use 360° video in a standard 16:9, 9:16 or 4:3 project.

When you load a 360° video into a standard 1:1, 4:3, 9:16 or 16:9 project, the entire 360° video will appear flattened – as in the standard view illustration on page 81.

However, PowerDirector includes a tool for selecting which area in the 360° video is displayed in your movie– essentially allowing you to create a normal-looking standard video from a selected view of the 360° video.

To designate the area of the 360° that will appear, select the clip on your timeline and, from the **Designer** Function Button that appears along the top of the timeline, select **View Designer**.

The **View Designer** that opens will display your clip with 360° navigation. However, the view you select by dragging your mouse over the video (or using the sliders along the left side of the pane) will be the *only* view that appears when the clip is used in your standard 4:3.,16:9 or 9:16 movie.

Using keyframes for the **Direction of View** controls (see **Keyframing** on page 126), you can even animate this view to change as the video clip plays.

Once your click **OK**, this video clip will function on your timeline like a standard 16:9, 9:16 or 4:3 video clip. (Although, of course, you can re-open the clip in the **View Designer** at any time and further adjust the view settings.)

The view you select of your 360 video can be set overall for the entire clip or can be varied throughout the clip using keyframes.

Blending Mode effects can be applied to a clip from the Effects Room.

Blending Modes

Blending Modes is a cool tool for creating interesting looks for your videos by combining elements of two videos or photos.

Blending Modes work by compositing your video with color or lighting effects from a selected template or another video. As with many features in PowerDirector, many **Blending Mode** templates are available with the program and many more are available for free from an ever-growing library on the **Director Zone** site, as discussed on page 86.

Your **Blending Mode** effect came be created using a template selected from the **FX Room** or by combing two videos layered on your timeline.

Apply a blending effect template

To apply a blending effect to your video, select a template from the **FX Room**. A number of templates appear in the **Blending** category. As with standard video effects, these effects can be dragged directly onto a clip on your timeline. These **Blending** effects include **Grunge, Lighten, Screen, Lens Flare** and **Light Leak**.

Blend two clips on your timeline

Blending Modes affect how the light, color and texture of a clip interact or combine with a video on a track below it on the timeline. **Blending Modes** create a composite look from two video clips, still photos or graphic patterns or designs.

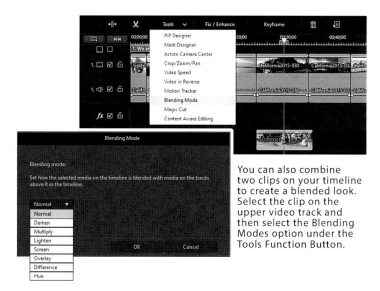

You can also combine two clips on your timeline to create a blended look. Select the clip on the upper video track and then select the Blending Modes option under the Tools Function Button.

To create a **Blending Mode** using two clips:

1 **Select and add a blending clip**

You can use any graphic design, still photo or even a video as a blending clip. Place your blending on your timeline on an upper video track so that it is positioned over the clip on your timeline you want to affect.

2 **Open the Blending Mode tool**

Select the clip you want to blend on the upper track of your timeline and, from the **Tools** Function Button along the top of the Timeline, select **Blending Mode**.

3 **Select a Blending Mode**

On the **Blending Mode** panel that opens, select a mode from the drop-down menu.

Blending Modes set how your upper track video affects the clip on the track below it. **Lighten** and **Darken** will blend either the lightest or darkest areas of the template with your video. **Difference** darkens the brightest pixel colors from your template and brightens to the darkest, blending sort of a negative image with your video. **Hue** blends in the template's colors. **Multiply** blends the darkest colors of your template while making the lightest transparent, while **Screen** blends the lightest colors while making the darkest transparent – and **Overlay** combines a little of each.

And if that seems rather difficult to fathom, don't worry too much about the technical definitions. **Blending** is best understood through experimentation: Test drive a couple of modes and see which one gives you the effect you want.

Download new Blending templates

The **DirectorZone** is an amazing resource for templates and effects. To browse available templates, click the **Free Templates** button. As we discuss on page 222, the **Director Zone** page includes a massive library of free downloads in a variety of categories, the vast majority of which are contributed by fellow PowerDirector users.

To install an effect or template from the **Director Zone**, just click the **Free Templates** button in the **FX Room** and browse the online library.

When the download is completed, locate the downloaded file on your computer. The file will have a **dzbl** suffix.

Once the file has been downloaded, the **Effect Installer**, a program that PowerDirector has installed on your computer, will automatically open and install the effect, after which it will be forever available to you in the **Blending Effect Designer**. (If it does not, simply locate the downloaded file and double-click on it.)

Using the Multicam Designer

Synchronizing Clips

Selecting Camera Angles

Tweaking Camera Cuts

Editing Multicam Video on the Timeline

Chapter 7

Edit MultiCam Video

Cutting between camera angles

One of my favorite features in PowerDirector is a tool usually seen only in professional video editing software – the ability to cut between video taken from several camera angles of the same event.

As with most of its tools, PowerDirector makes the process intuitive and easy.

One of the most advanced tools in CyberLink PowerDirector is a tool for editing multi-camera video.

Multicam video is video in which two to four (or more) camcorders shoot the same event simultaneously from different angles.

With PowerDirector's **MultiCam Editing** tool, you can view all of your video sources at once, and then select which video source you want to appear in your movie at any given point.

1   **Open the MultiCam Designer**

To edit your multicam video, select **MultiCam Designer** from the program's **Plugins** menu.

On the **Multicam Designer** that opens, click **Import Video** and gather your project's video.

Up to four separate video sources can be displayed in the **Source Video** monitors on the panel's upper left.

You can import more video sources or replace video in this workspace by clicking the **Import Video** button at the top left of the panel or by clicking the **+** button on any of the four **Source Video** monitors.

Video can be imported from your hard drive or from the **Media Room**.

2   **Select your Audio Source**

Click the **Audio Source** drop-down menu below the **Source Video** monitors.

You can use the audio from one of your camcorders as your multicam's master audio or import a separate audio file.

3   Sync your videos and audio

Since all of your video sources are recordings of the same event, you'll want to synchronize them before you begin cutting between them.

Under the **Synchronization** drop-down menu at the top of the panel, you'll find a number of ways to sync your video sources.

If your camcorders were synchronized with exactly the same timecode or time settings, you can use the **Timecode** or **File Created Time** options. You can also sync to **Markers On Clips** or even **Manually**.

But in our experience, the **Audio Analysis Synchronization** option is very effective. (Assuming, of course, that all of your camcorders were recording simultaneous audio of the event.)

Once you've selected your **Synchronization** method, click **Apply**.

In order to align the synced videos, the **Multicam Designer** may add black to the beginnings or ends of some clips.

4   Select your initial camera angle

Select your initial camera angle by clicking on its **Source Video** monitor. Once selected, this **Source Monitor** will be outlined in blue and its video will display on the panel's main **Preview** window.

If your playhead is over an area of your timeline in which only one, two or three of your clips are available you'll, naturally, see only that or those **Source Videos** as available.

5   **Record your camera angles**

Play through your video and plan where you'd like your cuts to occur.

When you're ready, click the red dot **Record** button under the panel's **Preview Window** and, as the video plays, click to select the camera angle you'd like at that particular moment.

As you switch camera angles, the angles you've chosen will be recorded to the **Recording** track at the top of the timeline.

6   **Tweak your angles**

Once you've finished recording your camera angles, tweaking them is very easy.

To divide one camera angle recording into two, position the playhead over the angle recording you want to divide and then click the **Split** button on the upper left of the timeline.

Click to Split at the   Drag to slide cut
playhead's position.   between angles.   Right-click to replace camera angle.

To extend or shorten a camera angle on the **Recording** track, hover your mouse over the intersection of two angle recordings until you see a double-headed white arrow, as illustrated at the bottom of page 90.

Click and drag to slide the cut point between those two camera angles.

You can also replace a camera angle completely by **right-clicking** on the camera angle on the **Recording** track and selecting a different **Video Source**.

When you are happy with your multicam recording, click **OK**.

Your finished video will appear on your timeline as a series of short video cuts, indicated with "**MCx**", and a separate track.

Turn your multi-cam video into a Video Collage

As an alternative to producing your multicam project as a full-frame video, you can assemble your multicam video into a video collage.

To port your synced videos to the **Video Collage Designer**, click the **Produce as Video Collage** button in the lower right of the **Multicam Designer**.

More information on using the **Video Collage Designer** can be found on page 76.

Assemble a synced composite video with 100 track Multi-Cam Editing

In addition to the dedicated **Multi-Cam Editor** workspace, PowerDirector 19 allows you to sync up to 100 simultaneously shot videos on the timeline and then combine them in your video frame with a variety of effects.

In other words, in PowerDirector Ultimate, you can synchronize video of a concert, wedding or sports event shot from up to 100 different angles and then cut or fade between these clips or even combine several clips into a split screen collage effect.

1   **Place your video on your timeline.**

As an example, I've place the four simultaneously-shot videos of a wedding on my timeline – each video on a separate track.

2   **Select and sync your videos.**

Select the video clips you want to synchronize on your timeline either by dragging across your timeline or, to select all, selecting your **Timeline** and then pressing **Ctrl+a** on your keyboard.

The **Sync by Audio** button will become active on the upper left of the **Timeline**. Click on this button.

When several simultaneously-shot videos are placed on your timeline, PowerDirector can use their audio to synchronize them.

The program will analyze the audio from all of the clips on your timeline and then align the clips so that their video and audio are synced.

Because your videos are layered on top of one another and each fills the video frame, only the video on "top" (in my example, the video on the **Video 4** track) will be visible in the **Preview** window. But, by scaling, positioning, changing the opacity and removing video on the upper video tracks, you can reveal one or more of the lower video tracks – sort of like spreading a deck of cards out so that several cards can be seen at once.

Once your tracks are in sync, your upper tracks can be cut, trimmed, split or have various effects added to them in order to reveal video on the lower tracks.

3 **Slice and trim your videos.**

The simplest way to reveal videos on lower video tracks is to delete segments from video on upper tracks. You can do this by using the **Split** and **Trim** tools, as described on pages 62 and 61.

When you **Trim** video on one track of a synced project, the remaining segments of the video will remain in sync. When you **Split** and then **Delete** a segment, selecting the option to **Remove and Leave Gap** will keep your clips in sync.

4 **Change a clip's opacity.**

Opacity is the opposite of transparency. When you lower a clip's opacity on the timeline, you make it transparent or semi-transparent, revealing the clip or clips on tracks below it.

To change a clip's transparency, select the clip on your timeline an d click the **Keyframe** button along the top of the timeline. The **Opacity** level can be adjusted under the **Clip Attributes**.

By using **Keyframing** (see page 126), you can vary the level of transparency to cross-dissolve between video tracks.

Opacity levels can be keyframed to create a dissolve between camera angles.

The Magic Movie Wizard

The Magic Cut Tool

The Magic Motion Designer

Chapter 8

Magic Tools

Easy ways to create cool movies and effects

PowerDirector includes a number of Magic Tools – easy-to-use tools for selecting the best segments from a clip, adding pan & zoom motion paths to your photos and even automatically creating great-looking movies from your raw footage!

Magic Tools are so cool, even veteran editors sometimes enjoy using them!

Magic Tools are semi-automatic tools for accomplishing tasks and creating media for creating and editing PowerDirector sequences and movies.

Which tools are available depends on whether you have a video clip or still photo selected on your timeline.

Some tools can be used on more than one clip at once.

PowerDirector 19 Ultimate **Magic Tools** include:

The Magic Movie Wizard is a tool for creating a movie automatically, based on your media and preferences.

The **Magic Movie Wizard** can be launched from either the **Welcome Screen** or by selecting the option under the **Plugins** menu at the top of the program We show you how to use it in **Chapter 2, Make Simple Movies in Auto Mode**.

Magic Cut automatically trims your clip to remove unwanted characteristics, based on criteria you select.

The **Magic Motion Designer** (see page 98) creates animated pan & zoom motion paths over your photos.

Magic Cut

The **Magic Cut** tool will analyze a longer video clip and then automatically select its best segments, based on the levels of each criterium you apply.

The segments selected by **Magic Cut** will be added to your timeline as separate clips with transitions, if selected, between each clip.

1   **Select a video clip on your timeline**

The tool will work with any raw footage. However, since the tool's primary function is to remove unwanted footage, it works most effectively with longer clips that include a variety of shots of people and situations of varying quality.

Apply fade between cuts.   Add music.   Set criteria levels.   Preview results.

2   **Select the Magic Cut tool**

   Magic Cut is found under the **Tools** Function Button.

   The **Magic Cut** panel will open displaying two tabs: **Duration** and **Criteria**.

   Click the **Preview** button in the lower right of then panel at any time to test drive your **Cut**.

3   **Set your edited clip's duration**

   Under the **Duration** tab, the **Magic Cut** panel will display your original footage's duration and its proposed automatically-edited **Cut** duration.

   A drop-down menu offers options for setting which video transitions, if any, appear between the segments in your **Cut**.

   By clicking the **Add Music** button, you can replace the audio on your **Cut** with any music or audio on your hard drive.

   You can add several musical clips to your **Cut** – up to your original clip's duration.

   If you click the button in the lower left of the panel, you can set your **Cut** to **Fit Duration to Background Music** duration.

4   **Set the Magic Cut criteria**

   Under the **Criteria** tab, you'll find sliders for customizing the criteria the tool uses to produce your **Cut**.

   When you are happy with your **Cut**, click the **Apply** button.

Open Pan & Zoom for a photo from the Tools menu.

Apply a motion path template to your slideshow or open the Magic Motion Designer by selecting the User Defined option.

The Magic Motion Designer

The **Magic Motion Designer** is a simple and intuitive tool for adding pan and zoom motion paths over your photos. These motion paths can be added by using a selection from a library of automatic templates or by creating your own custom keyframed animation.

Note, however, that these motion path templates and the **Magic Motion Designer** will only be available when you have selected a *still photo* on your timeline. Motion paths over videos are created using the **Crop/Zoom/Pan Tool**, as described on page 127.

1 **Select a photo on your timeline**

The tool can be used on an individual photo on your timeline or its templates can be applied to all of your photos at once.

2 **Select the Pan & Zoom tool**

Click the **Tools** Function Button along the top of the **Timeline** and select **Pan & Zoom** or select **Pan & Zoom** from under the **More Features** Function Button and, under the **Edit** Image sub-menu.

The **Pan & Zoom** panel will open.

3 **Apply a Pan & Zoom template**

The **Pan & Zoom** panel includes two dozen motion templates. Select a **Pan & Zoom** template and click the **Apply to All** button the lower right of the panel.

The **Pan & Zoom** motion path template will be applied to all of the photos on your timeline. A cross-fade transition will also be added between each slide.

Once you have applied a **Pan & Zoom** template to your slides, you can open each in the **Magic Motion Designer**, where you can customize the motion path.

As an alternative to applying a template overall, you can select an individual photo on your timeline and, on the **Pan & Zoom** panel, click the **User Defined** option. This opens the photo in the **Magic Motion Designer** with no motion path pre-applied.

Define starting keyframe view.

4   **Create a starting keyframe for your motion path**

If you have applied a **Pan & Zoom** template to your slideshow, click to select an individual photo on your timeline and then click the **Motion Designer** button in the lower right of the **Pan & Zoom** panel.

Motion paths are created in the **Magic Motion Designer** by defining views of your photo, each represented by a keyframe on the **Timeline**. The **Designer** will create the animated movement between the views or keyframes (similar to the **Crop/Zoom/Pan** tool described on page 127).

Create a new keyframe and define ending view.

Your starting keyframe is added to the **Magic Motion Designer** by default and is represented by a red, diamond-shaped keyframe on the **Timeline**.

Duplicate last   Add keyframe   Delete keyframe   Duplicate next

When you position the playhead on this keyframe, corner handles will appear around your photo. Drag these corner handles to define the initial view for your motion path. This view will be previewed in the upper right of the **Designer**.

5   **Create an ending keyframe for your motion path**

Position your playhead on the **Designer's Timeline**, at the point you'd like your motion path to end.

Click the **Add Keyframe** button. A new red, diamond-shaped keyframe will appear on your **Timeline** and corner handles will again appear over your over your photo. Drag these corner handles to define the end view of your motion path.

The tool will create the motion and zoom animation between the keyframes.

Naturally, you can add as many keyframes as you'd like to your motion path. And you can modify an existing keyframe by positioning the playhead over the keyframe and then dragging again on the corner handles.

Advanced Color Correction and Grading

Adding and Modifying Effects

Using the Chroma Key Effect

Adding and Modifying Particle Effects

Keyframing Motion Paths, Effects and Animations

Creating Custom Masks

Chapter 9

Video Effects and Animations

Color tone and special effects

CyberLink PowerDirector includes a wealth of video effects and movie overlays.

Some adjust the look or change the style of your video. Others add elements or special effects to your movie.

There are lots of cool ways to add visual styles and special effects to your movie with CyberLink PowerDirector.

Some of these effects change the tone or mood of your movie. Some allow you to add fantasy elements to your movie. Some are overlays, which allow you to add cool animated graphics to your movie.

And with the power of **keyframing**, you can customize their motion, settings and behavior precisely at any given point.

Color Enhancements

CyberLink includes a number of professional-style, advanced tools for correcting, adjusting and grading your video's color and bringing out its details. These tools are accessed by selecting a clip on your timeline and clicking the **Fix/Enhance** Function Button.

All of these enhancements can be applied overall to a video clip or to your entire movie, or they can be keyframed so that they are applied at different levels at different points. (We discuss keyframing in greater detail on page 126.)

Edge Enhancement

Edge Enhancement is a tool for upscaling video. Upscaling uses CyberLink's amazing **TrueTheater HD** system to make standard resolution video look nearly as sharp as high-definition – and can make high-resolution video look nearly as sharp as 4K!

The **Edge Enhancement Degree** slider adjusts the intensity of this enhancement. And naturally, there is a limit to how much it can be applied before your picture starts to look overly sharp.

Color Adjustment

The **Color Adjustment** tool is a set of manually controlled enhancements including exposure, brightness, contrast, hue, saturation, vibrancy, highlight healing (which can recover some detail lost in an overly-exposed image), shadow (which can recover some detail lost in an under-exposed or dark image) and sharpness.

Color Enhancement

Color Enhancement is a simple tool for increasing or decreasing the color saturation (or intensity) of your video clip.

Color Match

Color Match will automatically apply consistent color levels to your movie, based on the color levels of a selected clip.

To use it, select a clip on your timeline to activate the **Function Buttons**, then click the **Fix/Enhance** button along the top of the **Timeline.** On the **Fix/Enhance** panel, check **Color Match**.

Click the **Color Match** button on the panel that opens to the right and then follow the prompts.

Split Toning

The **Split Toning** tool allows you to grade your video's color by setting the hue and saturation of its brightest and darkest areas. In other words, you can give your video a more golden, warmer tone by clicking the **Highlights** box and then selecting a more yellowish color from the color picker and complimenting it with a green or brown **Shadows** selection. Likewise, by selecting blues and reds, you can give your movie a more menacing look.

In the feature film industry, color grading is considered an art, with color toning frequently used to set the entire tone of a movie.

HDR Effect

The **High Dynamic Range (HDR) Effect** adjusts the lighting around the edges of objects and people in your videos in order to recover detail lost due to high contrast in the image.

In other words, if you've shot video on an especially bright day or you've shot a person or object in front of a bright background, adjustments made to the **HDR Effect** can brighten highlight and details that have gotten lost in the shadows. I've gotten my best results by adjusting **Glow/Strength** first to brighten the image and then fine-tuning the look by adjusting the other properties.

Color Presets and LUTs

Presets are pre-created **color grades** which can be applied to adjust the color temperature, tint and tone of your video. Using **Color Effects**, you can change the entire look and mood of your movie with just a couple of clicks.

To access your library of **Color Presets**, open the **FX Room** and select the **Color Preset** category.

The program comes more than 40 presets in 6 categories. And, if you set the category drop-down menu to **All**, you'll also find the option to **Download Presets** free from the **DirectorZone**. (For more information on the **DirectorZone**, see page 222.)

Among these **Color Presets** are effects for making your video look like an old home movie, a low-budget 1970s movie, a surrealistic dream, a Martian landscape or like it was shot on a sun-washed summer day.

To apply an **Color Preset** effect, drag the preset onto a clip on your timeline or to the **FX track** to overlay several clips or your entire movie.

To fine tune the look, further tweak your clip's **Color Adjustment**, as described on page 102.

In addition to **Color Presets**, you can use third-party **LUTs** to apply color grading to your videos**. LUTS**, or **Look-Up Tables**, are pre-programmed color grades which can be used to give your movies a truly professional, cinematic look.

You'll find **LUTs** available for download all over internet, and a Google search for "free LUTs" will find many at no charge (though many of the freebies will require you to subscribe to a newsletter or site to qualify for the files). Once you've downloaded a batch of **LUTs**, unzip them and then store them in a directory folder on your hard drive. (I keep mine in a sub-directory folder in my Documents library.)

To add an **LUT** to your **FX Room** library, click the **Import** button at the top left of the **FX Room**, as illustrated above, and browse to the **LUT** file. (LUT files come in a variety of formats, including 3DL, CSP and CUBE.) The imported **LUT** will appear in the **FX Room**, in the **Color LUT** category. Once there, **LUTs** can be applied to your clip or your movie just as any other effect or **Color Preset**.

To remove an **LUT** or a **Color Preset**, select the effected clip on your timeline and click the **Effect** Function Button. On the **Effect Settings** panel that opens, uncheck or delete the **Color Preset** or **Look-Up Table** listing.

Video Effects

PowerDirector's library of video effects is found in the **FX Room**, opened by clicking the **FX** tab along the upper left of the program. A **Search the Library** box in the upper right of the **Room** allows you to do a real-time search for a specific effect.

PowerDirector includes over 100 video effects, including a package of effects from **NewBlue**, one of the world's top visual effects companies. The Ultimate and Director Suite versions include additional effects packages, and you can purchase even more effects from **NewBlue** by clicking on the **Download NewBlue Effects** button.

Many of these effects will add elements or particles to your video – like snow, fireworks, a lens flare, fire and smoke, bubbles, fog and rain. And a number of these effects are 3D, which means they'll appear 3-dimensional when used in a stereoscopic 3D project (see page 78).

Some effects will break up your video image, dividing it into a grid of several images or making it look like an Andy Warhol collage. Others will make your video look like a pen and ink, pencil or crayon drawing or make it appear to be reflected in a rippling pond. The program even includes a **Tilt Shift** effect, which we discuss in the sidebar on page 108.

Finally, there are a couple of **Text Masking** video effects. We'll show you how to use them on page 173 of **Chapter 12, Add Titles**.

You can, of course, preview an effect's look or animation in the **Preview Window** by clicking on its thumbnail in the **FX Room**.

Apply an effect

Effects can be applied directly to a clip or can be used as an "adjustment layer" (or applied to several clips at once) by adding them to the **FX track** on your timeline.

> **To add an effect directly to a clip**, drag it from the **FX Room** onto a clip on your timeline.

> **To add an effect as an adjustment layer,** drag the effect from the **FX Room** to the **FX track** on the **Timeline** – or select the effect and click the **Add to Effect Track** below the **FX Room** panel.

A selected effect can be dragged directly to a clip or added as an adjustment layer to the FX track by clicking on the Add to Effect Track button.

More than one effect can be applied to an individual clip. However, only one effect can be used as an adjustment layer over a given segment of your movie at a time.

When you add an effect to the **FX Track** as an adjustment layer (as illustrated above), the effect will be visible on every clip on the **Video 1 track** that is covered by the effect.

Once your effect has been added to the **FX track**, you can reposition it on the timeline or extend or shorten it by dragging on its ends.

An effect on the **FX track** can therefore be set to apply to only one clip, positioned to apply to a sequence of several clips – or it can be stretched to cover your entire movie.

Adjust your video effect

When a video effect has been applied to a clip, a small, orange "**i**" will appear on the clip.

> **To adjust or customize a video effect applied to a clip**, select the clip and click the **Effect** Function Button along the top of the **Timeline**.

> **To adjust or customize an effect on the FX track, double-click** on the effect or select the effect and click the **Modify** Function Button.

In either case, the **Effects Settings** panel will open.

Adjust an effect applied to a clip by clicking on the Effect function button.

Adjust an effect on the FX track by selecting it and clicking the Modify function button.

Every effect has settings that can be custom adjusted. If the playhead on the **Timeline** is over a clip to which the effect is applied, you will see the results of your adjustments in the **Preview** window.

A number of effects are animated and their settings change over time. For instance, the **TV Wall** effect, illustrated above, starts with a single image then, as the effect plays, it divides the video frame into more and more images. You should be able to see this by playing the effected clip or by scrubbing (dragging) the playhead across the clip or clips. This animation is created using **keyframes**. And when you attempt to make an adjustment to an animated effect, a panel will pop up advising you that "**This operation resets all keyframes in this effect. Do you want to continue?**"

In other words, making an adjustment to the effect will remove its preset animation. When you change the **TV Wall** effect to 15 horizontal and vertical squares, for instance, the effect will now display 15 horizontal and vertical squares *throughout the clip's duration*. The animation that zooms back from a single image to a grid of images will have been removed.

You can recreate this animation manually or create a custom animation from scratch for any effect by adding your own **keyframes** for the **Effects Settings**. We show you how to create and modify **keyframed animation** beginning on page 126.

The Effects Mask

Many video effects need not be applied to your entire video frame. Using the **Effects Mask**, you can isolate an area of your video frame and apply the effect to that area only.

We put the **Effects Mask** to work on **How do I blur a face like on TV's COPS** on page 227.

Disable or Remove effects

You can drag any number of effects onto a clip. And when you select this clip and click the **Effect** Function Button, the **Effects Settings** panel will display the list of effects applied, as illustrated above.

Select any effect to adjust its specific settings.

Uncheck an effect to temporarily disable that effect.

To remove an effect completely, select it and click the ━ button below the list.

The Tilt/Shift effect

A trendy but still pretty cool visual effect is the **Tilt/Shift**. The **Tilt/Shift** effect applies a blur to the top and bottom thirds of your video. When applied to footage shot from an oblique angle (about 45 degrees above ground level, with a close foreground and distant background), the result is a video that appears to have an extremely short depth of field – which makes your real-life scene look as if it were composed of toys or miniatures!

One of the most effective uses of the **Tilt/Shift** effect I've seen is a clip created from a time-lapse video of Disney World. You can see it at www.youtube.com/watch?v=HyZfIlxwsfl or by searching "Tilt Shift Disney" on YouTube.

Apply Chroma Key

To "key" a clip, in video editing, means to make it transparent. When you key a clip, you, for instance, replace the background behind an actor with a new background.

Chroma Key is the essential effect of fantasy and science fiction films – although it has lots of down to Earth uses too. For instance, on the nightly news, a weather forecaster is often shown in front of a moving weather map. In actuality, that forecaster is standing in front of a green backdrop, and the animation behind him or her is being added – or "keyed in" – electronically.

The **Chroma Key** effect can be used to place an actor shot in a studio in front of any real or imagined background in the universe.

The basic principle of **Chroma Key** is that footage of an actor or prop is shot in front of a flat-colored background (usually a green or blue background, since these colors are the opposite of human skin tones). This video is then placed over footage of a new background. When the green or blue background is made transparent, the actor appears to be in front of this new background.

To effectively use the **Chroma Key** effect, you will need two clips:

- A video of someone or some thing standing in front of a smooth, evenly-lit blue or green screen backdrop. We'll call this our **Foreground** video.
- A video or still image of a **Background** scene.

Although you can use a smooth, wrinkle-free sheet, blanket or even a wall as your backdrop, blue and green backdrop screens work best if they are bright and vivid. Bright, professional-style green or blue screens can be found online at sites like Amazon and filmtools.com for surprisingly little cost.

Good lighting is also crucial to creating a good key. Make sure your green or blue screen is well lit and without any shadows or hot spots – and make sure your foreground actor is lit separately and equally well.

Once you've got the parts, the rest comes pretty easy:

1   **Add your background to the Video 1 track**

    Place the video or still image that will serve as your new **Background** on the **Video 1** track, as illustrated on page 110.

    If you're using a video or photo that doesn't fill your video frame because it doesn't have the same aspect ratio, click to select the clip on your timeline and then drag on the corner handles that appear in the **Preview** window to enlarge your video or photo to fill the frame.

Background shot

Foreground or "key" shot.

2 Add your Foreground video to an "upper" video track

Place your **Foreground** video on **Video 2,** aligned with your **Background** clip. Ensure that the videos on both tracks are of equal length. (If you're using a photo as your **Background**, you can drag its end to extend it so that it's the same duration as your foreground video.)

Remember that, in PowerDirector, clips on **Video 2** will appear over clips on **Video 1,** even though **Video 2** is *below* **Video 1** on the **Timeline** itself.

3 Open the PiP Designer

Double-click on the **Foreground** clip on **Video 2.** The **PiP Designer** will open with **Video 2** displayed, as illustrated below.

4 Enable Chroma Key

Click the triangular toggle under the **Properties** tab to open the **Chroma Key** properties. Check **Chroma Key.**

5 Define the key color

Click to select the eyedropper next to the color swatch above the color wheel. Hover your mouse over the clip's background and click to sample the background's color.

Most or all of your green or blue background should become transparent, revealing the background clip on **Video 1** behind your actor.

Use the eye dropper to sample
your background color.

Your green or blue background
will become transparent.

If necessary, you can designate
a second Key color as transparent.

Save.

The smoother and more evenly colored this clip's green or blue screen is, the easier it will be to get a good, clean key.

If your green or blue background doesn't disappear completely, adjust the **Color Range** and **Denoise** levels. **If necessary, as illustrated above, you can even designate an additional Key color to add to the transparent area**!

When you're satisfied with your key effect, click **Save**.

Masks and Garbage Mattes

Masks cut your video into various shapes by "masking" or making areas outside the selected mask transparent. They can also be used as "**garbage mattes**" to remove areas of **Chroma Key** shot where the edge of the backdrop shows or where the background has a blemish or wrinkle that just won't key properly.

To apply a mask to a selected clip, open the **Mask Designer** by selecting the option under the **Tools** Function Button. Select a **Mask** (a rectangle will do) and then drag on the **Mask's** corner handles in the **Preview** window to size and position it to mask the problem areas in your shot.

It's best to apply a "**garbage matte**" before enabling **Chroma Key.**

For more information on using the **Mask Designer**, see page 123.

Open the Motion Tracker under Tools.

Define the object to be tracked with the Selection Box. The track wil be set to begin at that point.

Click the Track button to track the moving object across your video frame.

Motion Tracking

PowerDirector includes the ability to apply **Motion Tracking** – to track the movement of a person or object in a video clip – and then to set a graphic, title or media clip to lock onto and follow that object's movement across your video frame. This tool can often be used, for instance, to lock a **Mosaic** effect to an object or person in order to mask or censor a face or image.

1 **Open the Motion Tracker**

   Open the **Motion Tracker** by selecting a clip on the timeline and, from the **Tools** Function Button along the top of the timeline, select **Motion Tracker**.

   The **Motion Tracker** panel will open.

   To create a **Motion Tracker** effect, first identify a moving object in your video frame. Ideally, this object should be distinct from the background and should remain fairly consistent in look and color throughout.

   Once you've identified and created a **Tracker** that follows your object, you'll assign an element to it – a graphic or small video clip, a block of text or an effect – and this element will follow the object's movements.

   In my sample clip above, I'm tracking the movement of a jet over a runway.

2 **Define the object to be tracked**

   Position the playhead on the panel's timeline to the point you'd at which you'd like your **Motion Track** to begin.

   By dragging its corner handles, size and position the white **Selection Box** over the object you want to track. (The **Motion Tracker** assumes the point at which you've defined your object to be the beginning of your **Motion Track**, and it will automatically trim the blue-green **Tracker** overlay on the **Motion Tracker** timeline, as illustrated above.)

Lock a block of text, a graphic or video or a mosaic or spotlight effect to your Motion Tracked object.

3   **Track your object**

Click the **Track** button, as illustrated on the facing page. The program will track your object and, if it's done so correctly, the **Selection Box** will follow your object across your video frame. The track will continue as long as the object is visible and identifiable in the frame.

4   **Add a tracking element**

Select the option to add either a **Title**, a **Media Clip** or an **Effect**.

A **Title** will follow your object and, if you select the option to **Adjust Effect Size with Tracked Object,** the text will enlarge or shrink as the object tracks nearer or farther away. Once you've created and customized the text, drag it into position on or around the tracked object and it will remain in that position, relative to the object.

A **Media Clip** will appear as a picture-in-picture, which you can size and position relative to the tracked object. This clip can be a video or a still photo – and, if you are using a transparent PNG or even animated GIF file, as I did when I added the second jet, above, the opaque elements in the graphic will be visible and the transparency around the graphic will remain transparent.

You may also choose to lock a **Mosaic** or **Spotlight Effect** to the tracked object so that it either hides or highlights the selected object as it moves around the video frame. (We show you another method for masking or blurring an area of your video on page 216.)

In my example, I added a **Title** – the (fictional) name of the flight – which follows the jet's flight into the sky. Because I selected the option to **Adjust Effect Size with Tracked Object**, this title disappears into the distance with the jet.

If you click the **Add a Tracker** button, you can create one or more additional **Motion Tracks** on different objects on the same clip – each with its own **Title, Media Clip** or **Effect** added to it.

The Action Camera Center is a one-stop-shop for fixing, stylizing and enhancing video from sport (and other) camcorders. It includes a lens distortion fix and a library of stylish color grades.

The Action Camera Center

The **Action Camera Center** is a workspace that includes a number of tools for enhancing and correcting your video clips. The main purpose of the **Action Camera Center** is to provide a one-stop shop for working with footage from action cams – video from GoPros and similar sport or heavy-duty camcorders – although you can also use it with any standard camcorder footage.

Among the features included in the **Action Camera Center** is a tool for creating repeating **Time Shift** segments and a tool for adding a **Freeze Frame** to your clip.

The **Action Camera Center** is opened by selecting a clip on your timeline and then selecting the **Action Camera Center** option on the **Tools** Function Button, as illustrated above at the left.

Fix your clips

Under the **Fix** tab in the **Action Camera Center** are tools for correcting and enhancing the look of your selected video. Many of these same adjustments can also be found in the program's **Fix/Enhance** tools (see page 69). In fact, if a **Fix** is applied on either of these panels, the fix and its settings will be indicated in the settings on both panels.

Fixes in the **Action Camera Center** include the following, which are discussed in more detail under **Fix/Enhance** tools in **Chapter 6**:

Lens Correction. A fairly automatic tool that corrects distortion caused by the extreme wide-angle lenses on a number of sport cams, this advanced system includes correction presets for a number of **Makes** and **Models** as well as settings for fine-tuning the effect.

Video Stabilizer is a tool that takes a lot of the shake out of a wobbly shot.

White Balance is a set of adjustments for correcting white balance issues in your video. As we show you on page 69, an automatic way to correct white balance is to select the terrific **White Calibration** tool (eyedropper) and then use it to click on or "sample" a white area in your video.

Color Presets are a library of color grade presets that can be used to add style or a cool look to your video. (These are the same **Presets** available through the **Fix/Enhance** panel, as discussed beginning on page 103.)

The program comes with more than 40 stylish presets, including presets for making your video look like a 1960s home video or to make it look like it was shot on Mars. In addition to the nearly two dozen stock presets, you can also download many more for free from the **Director Zone** and, if you've got the **ColorDirector** add-on program, you can even create your own.

Create Time Shift effects

The **Action Camera Center** includes three tools for creating time shifts in your video.

The **Time Shift** tool can be used to shift your selected video segments into fast motion or, just as suddenly, pull them back to slow motion and back again. We show you how to use this tool in our discussion of the **Video Speed Designer** on page 72.

The **Replay** and/or **Reverse** tool sets a selected **Time Zone** segment of your clip to suddenly replay or reverse, as we discuss below.

The **Freeze Frame** tool briefly freezes your video's playback.

To Replay and/or Reverse a segment of your video.

1   **Create a Time Shift segment**

    Position your playhead to the point on your timeline you'd like your **Replay/Reverse** to begin, then click the **Create Time Shift** button at the top left of the timeline or on the **Effect** panel. (Either button will work.)

2   **Select the option to Replay/Reverse**

    Check the **Apply Replay and Reverse** option and set the number of times your selected segment will **Repeat**.

Create a Time Shift segment (indicated as a yellow overlay on the timeline).

Set the number of times the segment will repeat and if it will reverse before each repeat.

Note that adding time shifts and repeated segments changes the duration of the clip in your movie.

If you select the **Add Reverse Effect** option, the selected video segment will play, then reverse, then replay up to the number of **Repeat Times** you've set.

If you do not select the **Add Reverse Effect** option, your video will play, repeat the segment as set, then continue.

Speed Effects can also be added to your **Replay/Reverse** segment. See page 72 for more information on applying a **Speed Effect**.

To add a Freeze Frame to your video clip.

1   **Select the frame you want to freeze on**

Position the playhead on the frame in your video you'd like to freeze. Click the **Add Freeze Frame** button at the top left of the timeline or on the **Effects** panel. (Either button will work.)

A small marker along the top of the timeline will indicate the frame you've chosen to freeze. This marker is yellow when selected.

2   **Set your Freeze Frame attributes**

You may need to scroll down the Action Camera Center's **Effects** panel to see the **Freeze Frame** options.

Set a **Duration** for your **Freeze Frame**.

Optionally, toggle on the **Zoom Effect**. This effect adds a bit of interest to your **Freeze Frame** by suddenly zooming in and out of the area of the frame you indicate.

Note that adding a **Freeze Frame**, like adding a **Time Shift**, will change the overall length of your video. In other words, adding a 2-second freeze frame will make your clip 2 seconds longer than it was before. This means that, if the clip you're adding the **Freeze Frame** to is part of a movie on your timeline, the rest of the movie will ripple right to allow for the now longer the clip.

Click to Add a Freeze Frame, which will be indicated with a little marker on your timeline.

Set the duration the frame will hold.

Optionally, Apply a Zoom Effect and indicate the area that will be zoomed into/out of during the freeze.

Freeze Frames, like any time shift, change the duration of your clip on the timeline.

Particles can add animated effects like snow, fireworks, lens flares and shooting stars to your movies.

Add a Particle effect

PowerDirector's library of **Particle** effects is found in the **Particle Room**, available by clicking the **Particle** tab along the upper left of the program.

Particles are very cool special effects overlays that can add new elements to your movie scenes. Among the **Particle** effects available are clouds, bubbles, flares, shooting stars and pixie dust, fire, fireworks, snow and lots of interesting waves and trails. A **Search the Library** box in the upper right of the **Room** allows you to do a real-time search for a specific effect.

Most particles include transparency so that you can use them to add special animated effects over your videos!

The Stardust Particle effect.

Included in this set are CGI effects for adding rain, snow and fog to your movie's scenes! And particles can be personalized and customized.

Particle clips in the **Particle Room** are tagged to categories, although you can also select **All Content** to see them all at once. When you click on a particle, you'll see its animation in your **Preview** window.

Among these **Particles** are a number of elements that will appear as stereoscopic 3D when added to a 3D project. But even those that do not include 3D objects can be modified so that they have depth and dimension when used in a 3D movie.

In addition to the default set of **Particles** included with PowerDirector, additional **Particle** sets can be purchased from CyberLink by clicking the **More Premium Effects** link in the upper left of the panel.

117

Drag the Particle effect to an available video track or click Insert on Selected Track.

Apply a Particle effect

Particles can used as-is on the **Video 1** track – or they can be added to an "upper" video track (**Video 2, Video 3**, etc.), in which case they will overlay all of the video clips on **Video 1** or other lower video tracks.

A number of the **Particles** include **alpha**, which is a fancy name for transparency. The transparent areas of your **Particles** show as black in the **Particle Room** – and will appear as black if used on the **Video 1** track.

Particle clips that are not transparent (like **Planet, Star, Light, Flare, Bubble**, etc.) can be easily modified to make them transparent so that they can be used as foreground effects over your existing video, as discussed on page 119.

To add a **Particle** effect to your movie, either:

Drag the Particle from the Particle Room to an empty spot on your timeline. To use the **Particle** as an overlay or a foreground element, position the **Particle** clip on an upper video track. Or,

Select the track on your timeline you'd like to add the Particle clip to and position the **Timeline** playhead where you'd like the **Particle** clip to appear. Click the **Insert on Selected Track** button, as illustrated above.

If you add a **Particle** clip to an area of your timeline in which a clip already is placed, you will be prompted to select an overwrite or insert option, as discussed on page 60.

Particle clips are by default 10 seconds long. You can extend or trim your **Particle** clip to whatever length you'd like. If your **Particle** is animated, the animation will speed up or slow down to match the duration of the clip. In other words, if you extend your 10-second **Particle** clip to 20 seconds, the animation will appear at half its default speed. This, like every characteristic of a **Particle** clip can, of course, be modified in the **Particle Designer**.

Particle clips are made up of objects, some animated and some that emit animated particles.

Create or modify a Particle

Every **Particle** effect can be customized, either in the **Particle Room** or on your timeline. If you customize a **Particle** clip while it's still in the **Particle Room**, you'll be prompted to save it as a new custom **Particle**, and it will be available for your use in any future project.

If a modification is made to a **Particle** clip on your timeline, on the other hand, it will only affect that particular usage of the **Particle**.

To open the **Particle Designer** so that you can modify a **Particle, double-click** the **Particle** in either the **Particle Room** or on your timeline.

Make a non-transparent Particle transparent

In the **Particle Designer,** the individual objects or elements that make up a **Particle** clip can be disabled or removed completely.

To make a **Particle** clip that includes a **Background** transparent, uncheck the box on the track header of the **Particle Designer Timeline** track that includes the **Background** object – or select the **Background** clip itself on this timeline and delete it.

Once you've removed your **Background** track, you'll also have the option of adding your own custom background image.

To do so, click the **Set Background** button above the **Preview** window.

Disable or delete a Background.

Add a new background image.

Add Default Background Image

Add Custom Background Image

The **Particle Designer** is a workspace for customizing your **Particle** clip by adjusting the properties or characteristics of the particle objects, adding new particle objects, adding or changing a particle's animation and controlling the animation's timing.

To customize a particle object:

1 **Select the particle object**

 Particle clips are made up of one or a number of particle **objects**. Each object is represented as a clip on the **Timeline** below the panel's **Preview** window.

 Click to select an object clip on the **Particle Designer's Timeline**. When you do, the object will be indicated on the panel's **Preview** window as either an orange circle (if it is a stationary object) or a green line (if it is animated), as illustrated below.

2 **Set the object's properties**

 Particle Properties include an **Emit Method** (the shape of the particles emitted), a **Particle Style** (the pattern of the particles' movements) and controls for setting the object's color and other parameters. Some of these parameters can be pretty high-level, and they include settings for how many particles are emitted from your object, how long they last, how much they vary in size, etc.

 Again, remember that an object is only one element in your **Particle** clip, and some **Particle** clips include a number of animated and stationary objects on their **Timelines**.

 At the bottom of the **Properties** panel are checkboxes for setting whether the object fades in and/or out or merely appears in the **Particle** clip.

 Objects can also be temporarily turned off or disabled so that you can focus on one object at a time. To disable an object, uncheck the box on the track header of the track where the object appears on the panel's **Timeline**.

Selected object's properties.

Object's motion across the video frame.

Motion path applied
to selected object. Path creates Motion keyframes for the object.

3   **Select a motion path**

With the object selected, click to select the **Motion** tab. This will give you
access to a library of pre-created motion paths.

To apply a path to a selected object on the panel's timeline, click on your
selected **Motion** path, as illustrated above.

This path will be added to your object and will appear as a keyframed
property below the object on the **Particle Designers Timeline**.

Keyframes are tools for creating custom animations, and they appear
throughout the program. Keyframes, including those on this panel, be
easily created and modified.

**You can speed up or slow down any object's motion by dragging
the keyframes closer together or further apart.** The closer these little
diamond-shaped keyframes are on the timeline, the faster your animation
will happen.

We discuss keyframing in more detail on page 126.

4   **Add another animated object**

To add a new animated object to your **Particle** clip, click the **Add New
Particle Object** button above the **Preview** window.

A new track will be added to the panel's **Timeline** and a generic particle
object will appear on this track as a stationary object (with animated
"particles" emitting from it).

When you select the Add Image option, your new image will be added to a new track on the panel's timeline. By default, this new object will have Fade In and Fade Out applied to it.

If you select this object, you'll have the option to customize its **Properties** and **Motion** as discussed in **Step 2** and **Step 3**.

5   **Add custom images to your Particle clip**

To add a new custom object or image to your **Particle** clip, click the **Add Image** button above the Preview window.

A new track will be added to the panel's timeline and your still image will appear on this track as a stationary object.

If you select this object, you'll have the option to customize its **Motion** as discussed in **Step 3.**

Non-square objects

If you add a TIF or JPEG to your particle (or to your movie) as an object or you add an image to your movie or as a **Particle** object, it will most likely come in as a rectangular image – even if the graphic itself is, as illustrated above, non-square in shape.

In order to add your non-square graphic to your movie without the rectangular background, you'll need to create a graphic with no background layer in a program like Photoshop or PhotoDirector, and then save it in a graphic format that supports alpha, or transparency.

PNGs and GIFs are the two most popular formats for saving graphics with alpha channels.

Shape your video with a mask

The **Mask Designer** gives you the ability to use patterns as "cookie cutters" to cut your video into various shapes – including text shapes.

1   **Open the Mask Designer**

To open this workspace, select a clip on your timeline, click the **Tools** Function Button along the top of the timeline, then select **Mask Designer**.

The **Mask Designer** includes a library of basic shapes, including a rectangle, circle, heart and splash as well as a couple of cloud shapes that could be used to make your clip appear to be inside a thought bubble.

2   **Apply and adjust a mask**

To apply a mask shape template to your clip, simply click on it.

Below the mask library are settings for adjusting the **Feather Radius**, softening the edge of the mask. Under **Object Settings** you'll find settings for size, position, rotation and opacity of the mask as well as controls for using keyframes to vary these settings over the course of the clip.

You can also adjust the position and size of your mask by simply dragging over the mask and dragging on its corner handles in the panel's **Preview** window.

In addition to creating masks using the basic shapes on this panel, you can also load your own custom masks or even use text as a video mask, as discussed page 124.

Although the area outside of your mask shape may appear to be black in this panel, this area is actually transparent. In other words, if you use a mask on a clip on an upper video track, the video on the track or tracks below it will be visible outside the mask. A masked clip, then, can be used as a **picture-in-picture** over another video – or, if you use a cloud- or oval-shaped mask, it can be placed over another video and used as a thought or speech bubble!

For information on creating **picture-in-picture** effects, see page 148.

A masked video can be used as an interesting, non-square picture-in-picture.

Clicking
Create Mask
opens the
Mask
Composer.

3   **Load a custom mask image**

To use a custom shape for your mask, click the **Create an Image Mask** button below the library mask library and browse to an image on your hard drive. Almost any image format will work as a mask, although ideally the shape should be composed of pure black and white. Your video will appear through the white areas of your shape while the black areas of the image will be masked.

4   **Create text-shaped mask**

To create a mask in the shape of a title, click the **Create a Text Mask** button. This will open the **Mask Composer** (illustrated above), which looks very much like the **Title Designer** except that your video will show through whatever text you provide.

Type over the default "My Title" text with your custom title. Select a font, size and alignment for your title. Naturally, you'll get the best results if you use a heavier, thicker font.

Below the **Font** settings are **Object** settings for controlling the size, position, rotation and opacity of the title mask – although, as with controls in the **Mask Designer**, you can also change the size, position and rotation simply by dragging on the title in the **Preview** window.

5   **Create a Brush Mask**

To create a custom mask, click the heart-shaped **Create a Brush Mask** button. The **Brush Mask Designer** will open. In this workspace you can draw or paint your own custom mask shape.

As with standard masks, the area outside the text mask, although appearing to be black your mask is actually transparent. When your text mask is used on an upper video track, video on the track or tracks below it will display outside your mask.

Select the Custom Selection Mask.

Draw the vector using points. Use the Bezier tool to round the corners.

Move the playhead and reshape or reposition the vector to animate the mask's shape.

Create a vector-based Custom Selection Mask

In addition to being able to use a template or create a mask shape based on text or a painted area, as discussed on pages 123 and 124, PowerDirector 19 Ultimate's **Mask Designer** includes a tool for creating a **Custom Selection** vector mask. Vector shapes are defined by a series of dots which the program connects. Using keyframes, vector masks can even be animated to change shape or follow an object in your video clip.

1   **Select Custom Selection in the Mask Designer**

Click the **Custom Selection Mask** button under **Mask Properties**. Your video will appear grayed-out in the panel's **Preview Window**.

2   **Create your vector mask shape**

Click to add the dots that will define your mask's shape. When you complete your shape by clicking on your first point, your mask will be revealed. The dots you use to create this vector shape include a Bezier curve tool. Click on a dot and drag the Bezier handles that appear on either side of it to round out your shape's corner.

A diamond-shaped keyframe will appear at the position of the playhead, next to the **Mask** listing on the **Mask Designer's** timeline.

3   **Create a mask animation**

Move the playhead and reshape or reposition the points defining your mask's shape. A new keyframe will be created on the timeline and the **Mask Designer** will create the animation from the mask's shape to shape or position to position.

Add as many keyframes as you need to reshape your mask or to follow an object or person in your video.

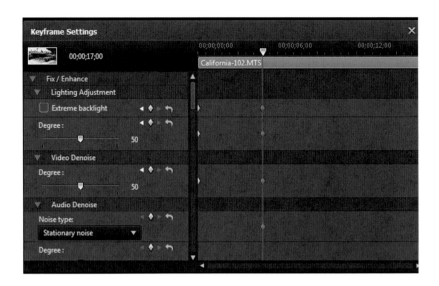

Keyframing

Keyframing is one of the most powerful tools in the PowerDirector toolkit. In fact, you'll find it represented throughout the program.

Keyframing can be used to create custom animations or motion paths, or to create effects that change characteristics or properties' settings over the course of a clip. Keyframes are also used to vary audio levels on your clips so that you can, for instance, mix several audio sources, raising and lowering their volume levels as needed (as discussed beginning on page 132).

The basic principles of keyframing are fairly simple. And once you learn them, you'll see keyframing throughout the program and you'll find yourself able to create all kinds of cool animations and effects.

Keyframes are little diamond-shaped markers that are added to a clip's timeline. Each keyframe represents a different setting for an effect, level or position. And, as you add keyframes to a clip's timeline, the program will create the animation or transition between these settings.

The **Keyframe Settings** panel, illustrated above, can by opened for any selected clip by clicking on the **Keyframe** Function Button along the top of the timeline.

Keyframed animation can be created on this panel for **Fixes/Enhances**, like color adjustments and white balance (as discussed on page 70); **Clip Attributes**, like position, scale and rotation; and audio **Volume**.

After you've added effects to your clip, these **Effects** will also appear here and, using keyframes, you'll be able to vary the settings for the effect over time – setting, for instance, a **Blur** effect applied to a clip to go in and out of focus. For more information keyframing effect's settings, see page 129.

Keyframe a Crop/Zoom/Pan

On page 74, we showed you how to use two keyframes added to the **Black and White** effect to create a video clip that transitions from black & white to color. On page 64, we showed you how keyframed **Opacity** levels create **Fade Ins** and **Fade Outs**.

To demonstrate further how keyframes work, we'll create a simple pan & zoom motion path over a video using the **Crop/Zoom/Pan** tool. (The process will be similar to the motion path we created over a photo using the **Magic Motion Designer** on page 98.)

1   Open the Crop/Zoom/Pan tool

Select a video clip on your timeline and click the **Tools** Function Button and select the **Crop/Zoom/Pan** option.

The **Crop/Zoom/Pan** panel will open.

Below the **Preview** window on this panel is a timeline representing the duration of your video clip. A red, diamond-shaped keyframe appears by default at the beginning of the timeline.

When the playhead is positioned directly on the keyframe, a rectangular overlay will appear over your video. This overlay indicates the view of your video this keyframe represents.

When the playhead is on a keyframe, any adjustments you make to the view will be applied to the keyframe.

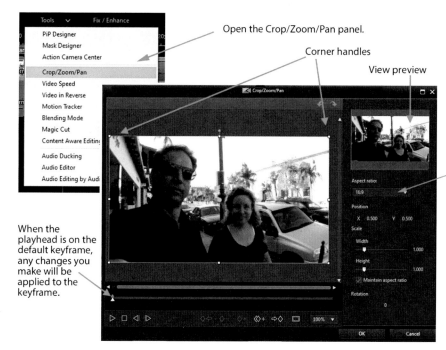

Open the Crop/Zoom/Pan panel.

Corner handles

View preview

Set Aspect Ratio to pan and zoom to an area that's other than the shape of your video frame.

When the playhead is on the default keyframe, any changes you make will be applied to the keyframe.

2 Adjust a keyframe

Drag the corner handles in or out to resize the view on your video. (Remember, the smaller this rectangular overlay, the larger your video will appear.)

Drag the center blue dot to change the rectangle's position.

Drag over the green dot at the top to rotate the rectangle.

3 Add a keyframe

Move the playhead to a new position on the panel's timeline. You can manually "scrub" the playhead into position or use the **Previous Keyframe** and **Next Keyframe** buttons below the timeline, below right, to jump from keyframe to keyframe.

Click the **Add Keyframe** button below the timeline.

A new keyframe will appear on the timeline and the corner handles will again appear on the white rectangle. Use the corner handles to adjust the view.

The green arrow that appears from the rectangle's center indicates the motion path your crop animation will follow.

Click **OK** to save your motion path and close the panel.

Some additional information on **Crop Video** keyframes:

You can add as many keyframes as you'd like to a clip's timeline.

Previous   Remove   Add   Duplicate Next
Keyframe. Keyframe. Keyframe. Keyframe. Keyframe.

The closer your keyframes are together, the faster the animation will be between them.

Use the **Previous Keyframe** and **Next Keyframe** buttons (illustrated above right) to jump from keyframe to keyframe.

Click the **Remove Selected Keyframe** button to remove the keyframe positioned directly under the playhead. (The default keyframe at the beginning Timeline can be modified but not moved or removed.)

Go to next keyframe

Go to previous keyframe

Add keyframe

The individual characteristics of an effect added to a clip can be keyframed to vary intensity or create an animation.

Keyframe Settings for effects and enhancements

The **Keyframe Settings** panel can be opened three ways:

Click the Keyframe button on the Effects Settings panel. The **Effects Settings** panel is opened when you have selected a clip to which effects have been applied and you click the **Effect** Function Button along the top of the **Timeline** (as discussed on page 66).

Click the Keyframe button on the Fix/Enhance panel. The **Fix/Enhance** panel is opened when you select a clip on the timeline and click the **Fix/Enhance** Function Button (as discussed on page 70).

Click the Keyframe Function Button along the top of the Timeline when you have a clip on the timeline selected.

No matter which of these three methods you use, you get to the same **Keyframe Settings** panel. On this panel, you can create keyframed transitions or animations to any **Fix/Enhance** adjustment (**Lighting, Video Denoise, Audio Denoise, Color Adjustment** or **White Balance**) or to the settings of any **Effects** you've applied to your clip.

In addition, you'll find a keyframing timeline for making animations based on **Clip Attributes** like **Opacity, Scale, Rotation** and **Motion**. These are the same attributes you can keyframe in the **PiP Designer**, as we do on page 151. In fact, any keyframing you've created in the **PiP Designer** will be displayed on this keyframing timeline, and vice versa.

Additionally, you can use this panel to keyframe audio **Volume** for a clip.

Although, there is another – usually preferred – way to set audio volume keyframes and to mix your audio. We show it to you on page 136.

Adding Audio Clips to Your Movie

Mixing Audio with the Audio Mixer

Mixing Audio with Keyframes

Detecting Beats in Your Music

Adding Effects with the Audio Editor

Chapter 10

Audio Editing

Mixing audio and adding audio effects

As an element of your movie, your audio is at least as important as your video.

You want your projects to have good, clean audio – and you want this audio to have the same excitement and tone as your video.

Though not quite as feature-rich as its video tool set, CyberLink PowerDirector includes a number of terrific tools for creating, mixing and adding effects to your audio.

Additionally, all versions of PowerDirector come bundled with WaveEditor, a powerful audio editing program that works as a standalone audio editor as well as interfacing directly with your PowerDirector project.

Add audio and music clips to your timeline

Adding audio clips to your timeline is essentially the same as adding video to your timeline. You just drag your audio clips from the **Media Room** to an audio track on the **Timeline**. If you attempt to place an audio clip on a track where it will overlap another audio clip, you will work with the insert/ overwrite options, as illustrated above and detailed in page 60.

Like video clips, your audio clips can be trimmed and split (see pages 61-62). And, if you delete a clip from your timeline, you must choose from the same set of ripple options as you do when you delete video (see page 62).

Music, narration or other audio can placed on any audio track.

Mix your audio levels with keyframes

You'll often be mixing audio from several sources in your PowerDirector project. And, when you do, you'll want to properly mix this audio – ensuring that one audio source dominates, for instance, while the other audio sources play in the background or mute completely.

PowerDirector background music

PowerDirector Ultimate comes bundled with more than 50 royalty-free **Background Music** tracks in a variety of styles, as discussed on page 57.

A typical example of this is when you have three audio sources – the audio that's included with your video, a musical soundtrack and a narration track.

In this case, you'll likely want your musical track to dominate when there is no narration. And then, when the narration comes in, you'll want your music to temporarily fade back so that the narration can be clearly heard.

Mixing audio is usually best done with keyframes. **Keyframing** is a feature that you'll find throughout the program as a way to control and customize a number of effects and animations (as discussed on page 126).

Keyframing audio means setting audio levels at specific points in your movie – varying your volume levels as needed to properly mix your audio levels.

In the illustration above, I've assembled a short movie that consists of several video clips (with their accompanying audio), a music soundtrack and a couple of short narration clips.

View Audio Meters

The **Preview Window** can optionally display very helpful **Audio Meters** so you can more easily monitor your audio levels as your movie plays.

Remember, for best results you want your audio levels full and green and not peaking in the red.

The option for displaying the **Audio Meters** is found under the **Display Options** button along the bottom of the **Preview** window.

Because the audio on my video clips isn't relevant, I'm going to mute it completely.

Then I'll mix the voice and music tracks so that music fades down whenever the narration is playing.

There are a couple of ways to do this in PowerDirector: Adding keyframes with the **Audio Mixer**, as we discuss below; creating **Gain** keyframes right on the **Timeline**, as we discuss on page 136; and setting the audio levels on the **Keyframe Settings** panel, as we discuss on page 137.

The Audio Mixing Room

Vertical sliders, or Video Volume sliders, add keyframes to clips, setting the Volume levels at specific points in a clip.

Horizontal sliders, or Master Sliders, set Gain/Volume levels for all clips on the track at once.

Normalizer automatically adjusts the overall Gain level of a clip.

Adding keyframes with the Audio Mixer

This method uses the sliders in the **Audio Mixing Room** to keyframe your clip's **Gain** levels.

1 **Open the Audio Mixing Room**

PowerDirector's audio mixer can be opened by clicking the **Audio Mixing Room** tab along the upper left of the program.

This panel will display sliders for the **Timeline's** audio tracks. Tracks that have audio on them will be highlighted and active. (If the timeline's playhead is not over a clip on an audio track – say, it is between narration clips – that slider will also not be active.)

2 **Mute the Audio 1 track**

The easiest way to mute an entire track is to use the **Master Audio** slider in the **Audio Mixing Room**. This is the little *horizontal* slider below the track's vertical slider.

As you move this slider left for the **Audio 1** track, you will see the horizontal line that runs through *all audio clips* on **Audio 1** lowering. This horizontal line through your audio clips represents your clips' **Gain** level (essentially the audio clip's volume).

Sliding a Master slider to the left mutes the track completely.

Clicking on the slider handle or making adustments to the Gain slider creates new keyframes on your clip.

Raising and lowering these keyframes creates fades up and down.

Lowering the Master Gain slider lowers the Gain level for all clips on the track.

To mute an audio track, slide the **Master Audio** slider completely to the left as in the illustration above.

The reason this is a preferred way to mute the audio on a track is because, as opposed to, say, disabling the audio track (unchecking the **Disable/Enable** box on the track header) or muting the clips (by selecting the option on each clip's **right-click** menu), setting the master level simply reduces the overall **Gain** for the clips on this track.

If you need to, you can still drag the **Gain** level line up for a certain clip if you'd like to feature its audio.

3 **Add a keyframe to begin the fade down**

Position the playhead on the **Timeline** to just before first **Narration** clip begins.

On the **Audio Mixer**, click on the handle on the **Music** track's slider (but don't actually move it). This will add a little dot to the **Gain** line on your music clip. This dot, or keyframe, will be the beginning of our fade down.

4 **Add a fade down Gain keyframe**

Move the playhead to the very beginning of the **Narration**. Drag the **Audio Mixing** slider for the **Music** track down to reduce the gain level to about -8.0 (or type -8.0 in the **dB** box). This will create a new keyframe that is slightly lower on the music clip than the initial keyframe, as illustrated above.

5   **Add a keyframe to begin the fade up**

Move the playhead to just before the **Narration** ends.

In the **Audio Mixer**, click on the handle on the **Music** track's slider again (and, once again, don't actually move it). This will add another keyframe to the **Gain** line on the music clip. This keyframe should be at the same -8.0 dB level as the previous keyframe.

6   **Add the fade up Gain keyframe**

Move the playhead to just after the **Narration** ends. Move the slider in the **Audio Mixer** or type in numbers to set the **Music** clip's **Gain** back to 0.0.

A new keyframe will be added to the music clip, bringing the **Gain** level back to where it was before we faded it back.

The little "hammock" we've created between these keyframes will trigger the fade down, then fade back up, of the music clip as our narration clip is playing.

The -8.0 **Gain** level is, of course, just a general setting for your music's fade-back level. You can use whatever **Gain** level best mixes your audio.

Keyframes can also be created simply by clicking and dragging on the Gain level line.

Creating Gain keyframes right on the Timeline

Audio level, or **Gain**, keyframes can also be created right on the **Timeline** – and many people find this method the preferred way to mix their audio.

1   **Add keyframes to your music clip**

Click on the horizontal **Gain** level line that runs through the music clip. This will create a little dot – a keyframe.

Create a total of four keyframes – one just before the **Narration** starts, one just as the **Narration** starts, one just before the **Narration** ends and one just after the **Narration** ends, as illustrated above.

2   **Position the fade down keyframe**

Drag down on the second keyframe you created. An indicator will appear, showing you the **Gain** level you are setting. Drag it to approximately -8.0 dB.

Normalize your audio volume

Normalizing is an automatic way of correcting your clips' **Gain** levels.

When you click the **Normalize** button in the **Audio Mixing Room** (as illustrated on page 134), the program will analyze the **Gain** levels of your clips and, if necessary, raise or lower them to a "normal" level.

The challenge, of course, is that you may have loud and quiet audio in the same clip. **Normalizing** is an overall adjustment – and it will base its settings on the clip's loudest sounds. It will not compensate for variations in the sound levels on a clip.

3   **Position the begin fade up keyframe**

Drag down on the third keyframe you created. Drag it to approximately the same **Gain** level as you did the previous keyframe (-8.0 dB).

You should end up with the same "hammock" keyframe configuration as we did when we used the sliders in the **Audio Mixing Room**. The **Gain** level for the music fades down when the **Narration** clip is playing, then fades back up to its previous level after the **Narration** ends.

Setting audio levels with Keyframe Settings

A clip's **Gain** level can also be keyframed in the **Keyframe Settings** panel. To open this panel, select an audio clip and click the **Keyframe** Function Button along the top of the **Timeline**, as illustrated on page 138.

Click the little triangular toggle to the left of the **Volume** listing to open the volume settings slider and timeline.

To create **Gain** keyframes in this panel:

1   **Create a keyframe to begin the fade down**

Position the playhead on the panel's **Timeline** to just before where you'd like your fade down to begin. (The playhead on the program's main **Timeline** moves in sync with the panel timeline's playhead – so drag the playhead in the **Keyframe Settings** panel until the playhead on the main **Timeline** is just before the **Narration** begins.)

Add Keyframe.

Previous Keyframe.

Next Keyframe.

Click the **Add Keyframe** button on the **Keyframed Settings Timeline**. This will add a keyframe to the panel's **Timeline** as well as to the music clip on your main **Timeline**.

This keyframe will be the beginning of your fade down.

Keyframes in the Keyframe Settings panel correspond to keyframes on the clip itself.

2 **Add a fade down Gain keyframe**

Align the playhead with the beginning of the **Narration**. Drag the **Volume** slider to reduce the gain level to about -8.0 (or type -8.0 in the *dB* box). This will create a new keyframe that is slightly lower on the music clip than the previous keyframe.

3 **Add a keyframe to begin the fade up**

Move the playhead to just before the **Narration** ends.

Click on **Add Keyframe** button to create another keyframe. This keyframe should be at the same -8.0 dB level as the previous.

4 **Add the fade up Gain keyframe**

Move the playhead to just after the **Narration** ends. Move the slider or type in numbers to set the **Volume** back to 0.0 dB.

A new keyframe will be added to the music clip and on the panel's **Timeline**, bringing the **Gain** level back to where it was before we faded it back.

Keyframes can be dragged to new positions (left and right as well as up and down), as needed to tweak how and when they fade up and down the audio.

Remove a clip's audio keyframes

To remove all audio keyframes applied to an audio clip on your timeline, **right-click** on the clip and select **Restore to Original Audio Level**.

Mix your audio levels with the Audio Ducking tool

PowerDirector's **Audio Ducking** tool automatically mixes the audio in your movie, raising and lowering the volume level of a selected music track to allow the dialog to be heard in your video clips.

To apply **Audio Ducking**, select the music clip on your timeline and then, from the **Tools** Function Button along the top of the **Timeline**, select **Audio Ducking**.

The **Audio Ducking** panel that opens includes sliders for setting the sensitivity to your video's sound and the ducking levels your audio will be pulled back to. You can also control the fade in and fade out duration – how abruptly the program lowers the music track's audio level. When you click the **OK** button, the program will automatically create the necessary audio level keyframes on your music clip.

Audio Ducking mixes only the audio from your video clips with a music clip. It won't mix two audio tracks or lower the levels of your music clip to allow your narration to be heard. Which is why most professionals prefer mixing their movies' audio manually, using keyframes, as discussed in the first half of this chapter.

Record a Voice-Over or narration

PowerDirector includes tools for recording narration or a voice-over directly to your project's timeline.

To record narration or a voice-over:

1 **Open the Voice-Over Recording Room**

PowerDirector's recording workspace can be opened by clicking the **Voice-Over Recording Room** tab along the upper left of the program.

The Voice-Over Recording Room and Preferences.

Start/Stop Recording.

Fade In. Fade Out. Audio Input Level slider. Mute audio while recording.

2   **Configure your microphone**

If a microphone is operating on your computer, the little microphone icon on this tab should be highlighted.

If it is not, you will need to ensure your microphone is properly configured in Windows.

If you have more than one microphone attached to your computer (say, for instance, you have a microphone on your webcam in addition to your recording microphone), make sure that the correct device is configured for your **Voice-Over**. Click the panel's **Device** button and select your recording microphone from the **Audio Device** drop-down menu, as illustrated.

The **VU meter** on the left side of the panel will show the level of your microphone's input.

Speak or read into your microphone and ensure that VU shows a full green line but does not peak out at red. A red VU is an indication that your microphone is too "hot", and this could result in distorted audio.

Use the **Audio Input Level** slider to set a good level for your voice.

Click the **Preferences** button to set up your recording preferences. Among the choices on this panel is the option to precede your recording with a 3-second countdown.

If you don't select this option, recording will begin immediately when you click the **Record** button.

You also have options to limit the length of your **Voice-Over** and to add a fade in or out at the beginning and/or end of your recording.

You can also add a fade in or fade out to your recording manually by clicking the buttons below the **Audio Input Level** slider on the panel, as in the illustration on the facing page.

3   **Record your Voice-Over**

Position the playhead on the **Timeline** at the point you'd like your **Voice-Over** to begin.

Use the **Mute All Tracks When Recording** checkbox on the panel to set whether you do or do not want to hear your movie as you're recording your **Voice-Over**.

Click the red dot **Record** button and, unless you've set the 3-second countdown preference, immediately begin your **Voice-Over**.

4   **Stop recording**

When you're finished, click the red dot **Record** button again to stop recording. The program will process and save your recording and then add it to your timeline.

Detect beats in your music

Among the cool audio features in PowerDirector is a tool for automatically detecting the beats in a musical clip. Detected beats can be used as a great reference for, say, creating a slideshow or adding video clips that cut to the rhythm of a song.

To use the **Automatic Beat Detection**:

1   **Ensure the Detect Beats track is visible**

The **Clip Marker Track** is an optional track that runs along the top of the **Timeline**.

To enable it, **right-click** on the **Timeline's** track headers and, in the context menu, check the **Show Clip Marker Track** option.

Ensure the Clip Marker Track is enabled, then right-click on your music clip and select Automatic Beat Detection.

Detect Beats   Beat Markers   Zoom   Manually Add Beats   Remove Beat Markers

2   **Launch Auto Beat Detection**

    Right-click on a music clip on your timeline and select the option to **Use Automatic Beat Detection**.

    The **Automatic Beat Detection** panel will open, as illustrated at the top of the facing page. Your musical clip will be represented as a waveform on the panel's **Timeline**.

3   **Detect beats**

    Click the panel's **Detect** button. The program will analyze your music and create a series of beat markers above the panel's timeline.

4   **Test drive the beat markers**

    Click the **Play** button on the panel's timeline and evaluate how well the tool has tracked the beats. You may want to **zoom** in on the timeline so that you can better see the individual beat markers.

    If you're happy with the results, click **Apply**.

As an alternative to **Automatic Beat Detection**, you can manually add beat markers to your clip.

To do this, click the **trashcan** icon in the upper right of the **Automatic Music Beat Detection** panel to remove the current keyframes. Then play the music and click on the **Add** button in rhythm with the music. (As an

When you add or trim a clip on your timeline, the cut will "snap" to the beat marker.

alternative, you can click the **Add** button to create the first beat marker, then tap the "**a**" key on your keyboard to create the rest.)

When you're happy with the results, click **Apply**.

The beat markers will appear on the **Clip Marker (Music Beat) Track** at the top of the **Timeline**. These markers are assigned to the music clip they detected beats for. If you drag the music clip to another position on your timeline, the markers will follow it.

These markers also create invisible "snap-to" guides on the **Timeline**.

When you add or trim a clip on your timeline, the beginning or end point of the clip will "snap" to the marker's position.

Add audio effects with the Audio Editor

PowerDirector Ultimate includes a powerful editor for cleaning up and enhancing your movie's audio. The **Audio Editor** can be used to remove noise, add dynamics, equalize or add special effects to your audio.

Open a PowerDirector clip in Audio Editor

Select an audio clip or a video clip that includes audio on your timeline.

Select **Audio Editor** option from the **Tools** Function Button.

The **Audio Editor** will open and the audio from your selected clip will appear as a waveform in it, as illustrated on page 144.

An important thing to note about this audio, however: **This is audio from the clip** *as it appears on your Timeline.*

In other words, if you have a longer clip that's been trimmed on your timeline, only the trimmed segment – the segment of the clip that actually appears on your timeline – will open in the editor.

Audio adjustments and effects can be applied to an entire clip or limited to a selected range.

In the **Audio Editor**, you can add your **Effects** to all or a portion of this clip.

> **If you do not have a Range selected in this clip**, your **Effect** will be applied to the entire clip.

> **If you have a Range selected** (highlighted in yellow, as in the illustration), the **Effect** will only be applied to that segment.

To apply an effect, select the **Effect** from the listing along the left side of the **Audio Editor**.

When you apply an effect, an option screen will open in which you can set various levels for the effect. If you check the **Preview** box at the bottom of a panel, you'll be able to test drive the effect and your settings.

Among the audio effects available are:

> **Volume**, which includes **Dynamic Range Compression,** which limits audio levels, reduces the difference between the loudest and quietest sounds in your audio and uses a "gate" to remove unwanted, low-level noise.

> **Distortion**, which can be used to change the pitch of a voice or sound or transform the entire tone of an actor's voice.

> **Adjustments**, which includes an **Equalizer** for fine tuning the levels of your audio at various frequencies of bass, midrange and treble.

Effects can be applied to the entire clip or to a selected region only (highlighted in yellow-green). To test drive an effect's settings before applying them, check the Preview box at the bottom of the effect's option panel.

Generate, which includes the **Reverb** effect for creating echoes as well tools for replacing portions of your audio with silence or a buzzing noise.

Special Effects, which include tools for reducing noise in your audio, as well as tools for making your audio sound as if it's coming from a cheap radio, a telephone or speaker phone. You'll also find a **Vocal Eraser** tool in this set of tools for removing vocals from songs in order to create your own karaoke music.

Naturally, you can add more than one effect to a clip at a time.

Creating Picture-in-Picture Effects

The PiP Designer

Working with Multiple Tracks of Video

Using and Creating PiP Objects

Animating Lines in the Paint Designer

Working with Sketch Animations

Chapter 11

PiPs and Multi-Track Video Effects

Working with layers of video

Many cool visual effects can be created by layering video on top of video.

With 100 video and audio tracks available, PowerDirector offers lots of opportunities to create interesting picture-in-picture and other multi-track effects.

Compositing is the process of combining several tracks of video to create a visual effect.

When video clips are placed on separate tracks above one another, they behave as if in a stack. The clip on the top track is the most visible, with the clips on tracks below it visible around and through transparent areas in it.

Multi-track video effects include **Picture-in-Picture** effects, **Chroma Key**, J-cuts and L-cuts and video grids (like what we call the "Brady Bunch effect").

Create a Picture-in-Picture effect

A **Picture-in-Picture** composition is a video in which one or more smaller videos are overlayed onto a main video as an inset or as a smaller video visible in the corner of the screen.

There are two ways to create **Picture-in-Picture** effects: You can create the effect directly on the **Timeline**, or you can use the very powerful **PiP Designer**.

Create a Picture-in-Picture effect on the timeline

The simplest way to create a **Picture-in-Picture** composition is to layer a video over another video on your timeline, and then resize and re-position the upper track video using tools right in the program's **Preview** window.

1   **Place your video clips**

Place your main or background video on the **Video 1** track. Place the video you will use as your **Picture-in-Picture** (PiP) on the **Video 2** track, overlaying it, as illustrated at the top of the facing page.

Remember that, in PowerDirector, the track layers are represented by default on the **Timeline** "upside-down." In other words, videos on **Video 2** will appear *over* videos on **Video 1** in your movie, even though on the **Timeline** itself they are placed *under* them.

Because the PiP video clip on **Video 2** currently fills the video frame, you will only see this video in the **Preview** window at this time.

Chroma Key

Chroma Key is a powerful multiple track effect in which you take a video of an actor and replace its background with any real or fantasy background.

For more information on this cool tool, see **Apply Chroma Key** on page 109.

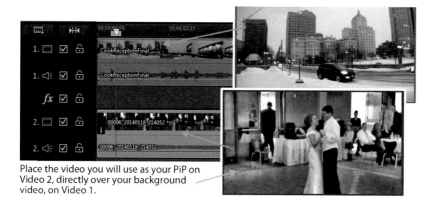

Place the video you will use as your PiP on Video 2, directly over your background video, on Video 1.

2 Resize the PiP video

Click to select the PiP video clip on your timeline. Corner handles will appear around the outside of this video in the **Preview** window, and a blue crosshair will appear over the video's center as illustrated below right.

Drag these corner handles in to resize the PiP video. This will reveal the video on **Video 1** behind it.

3 Position your PiP

Click on the blue crosshair in the center of the PiP video and drag the clip into position in your video frame.

When a clip is selected on your timeline, you can scale and position it by dragging on the corner handles and center point in the Preview window.

Several layers of video tracks can be used to create as many PiPs as you'd like (or a grid, as we show you on pages 154-155). Just select the clip you want to resize and reposition on the **Timeline** to activate its corner handles.

The scale and position of your **Picture-in-Picture** can also be animated using keyframes – an effect that can be created using the **Clip Attributes** in the **Keyframe Settings** window (see page 126) or by using the **PiP Designer** (as we show you on page 150).

Create a Picture-in-Picture effect in the PiP Designer

The **PiP Designer** is a powerful workspace for creating effects on multiple tracks or layers of video.

To open the **PiP Designer**, select a clip and click the **Tools** Function Button along the top of the **Timeline** and select **PiP Designer** – or simply **double-click** a clip on your timeline.

The **PiP Designer** includes a set of **Properties** tools for affecting how your PiP affects the clips below it and **Motion** tools for creating movement for your PiP over the clips below it.

Additionally, the **PiP Designer** includes tools for scaling and positioning your **Picture-in-Picture** video as well as a **Timeline** for animating these PiP settings.

Safe Zones

Whenever you're compositing images or text in a video frame, it's a good idea to work with the **TV Safe Zone** turned on in your **Preview Window**.

The **TV Safe Zone** is a rectangular guide that appears over your **Preview** window, indicating the area you should keep all of your text and relevant video in. This helps protect important parts of your video or text from being cut off when shown on a TV.

For more information on the **TV Safe Zone**, see the sidebar on page 175.

To create a **Picture-in-Picture** in the **PiP Designer**, begin with your background video on the **Video 1** track and the video you want to use for your **Picture-in-Picture** on V**ideo 2**, as illustrated at the top of page 149.

1   **Open the PiP Designer**

    Select a clip and click the **Tools** Function Button along the top of the **Timeline** and select **PiP Designer** – or simply **double-click** a clip on your timeline.

    The **PiP Designer** will open and the selected clip will appear in the panel's **Preview Window** with handles on each corner.

2   **Scale and position the PiP**

    Drag on the corner handles to change the PiP's size in the video frame – then click and drag it into position.

Animate your Picture-In-Picture in the PiP Designer

By default, the changes you make to the clip's **Scale, Motion, Opacity** and **Rotation** are made for the duration of the clip. In other words, if you position your PiP in the upper left corner of your video frame, it will remain in that position for the entire clip.

You can, of course, also **keyframe** animation for any of these properties so that your PiP changes size and position over the course of the clip.

For instance, let's take our PiP of the couple dancing in the upper left of the video frame and animate so that this PiP begins in this upper corner, then shrinks down and disappears in the center of the video frame.

1   **Create your PiP's initial position**

    Ensure that the playhead on the **PiP Designer** is at the beginning of the panel's **Timeline**.

    Drag your PiP's corner handles to scale and position the clip in the upper left of the video frame (as we discussed on the facing page).

2   **Create your initial keyframe**

    Click the white, diamond-shaped **Add Keyframe** button on the track headers for **Scale** and **Motion** (or whatever properties you plan to animate), as illustrated to the right.

    Diamond-shaped keyframes will be created at the position of the playhead on the panel's timeline.

Resize and position your PiP by dragging its corner handles.

Previous Keyframe

Add Keyframe

Next Keyframe

Click Add Keyframe to duplicate
previous keyframe settings.

Scale and reposition the PiP and the program
will automatically create new keyframes.

3   Create a second keyframe that duplicates the first's settings

Move the playhead a second or two down the panel's **Timeline**.

If we were to create a keyframe with different **Scale** and **Motion** settings at this position, the program would create an immediate transition from the first keyframe's settings to this keyframe's settings.

So, rather than beginning our animation immediately, let's create a second keyframe with the same settings as the first – so that our PiP will remain in its position for the first second or two of the clip.

Click the **Add Keyframe** buttons again for **Scale** and **Motion**. New keyframes will be created at the playhead's current position, as in the illustration.

4   Create a zoom out keyframe

Drag the playhead another second down the panel's **Timeline**.

Drag the PiP video into the center of the video frame. (A new **Motion** keyframe will be created automatically.)

Drag the PiP's corner handles in until the clip disappears completely, as on the facing page. Better yet, toggle open the **Object Settings** on the **Properties** panel, drag the **Scale** settings for **Width** and **Height** down to zero (technically 0.0001, the lowest setting possible).

We've now created an animation in which our PiP begins in the upper left corner of our video frame, stays there for a moment, then zooms out and vanishes into the center of our video frame.

For more information on creating animations, see **Keyframing** on page 126.

Interpolate PiP keyframes

A new feature of PowerDirector 19 is that keyframes added in the **PiP Designer** can now be interpolated.

In other words, if you **right-click** on a keyframe on the **PiP Designer** timeline you can set whether the program creates a smooth movement from setting to setting, whether it speeds or slows between keyframes or whether it holds a position or setting and abruptly changes when it reaches the next keyframe.

PiP Designer Properties

In addition to **Object Settings** for creating **Scale**, **Motion** and **Rotation** animations, the **PiP Designer** includes tools for creating a number of **Picture-in-Picture** effects.

Under the panel's **Properties** tab, you'll find settings for controlling and keyframing how your PiP is sized or positioned and how it reacts with the video clips that are under it on your PowerDirector **Timeline**.

Object Settings include settings for the **Position** of your video in your video frame, its **Scale**, **Opacity** and **Rotation**.

Chroma Key is an effect which creates transparency through your video clip, based on a color range you designate. We show you how to use this tool in **Apply Chroma Key** on page 109.

Border adds a border, or outline, around your PiP.

Shadow adds a drop shadow under your PiP. Settings control how far this shadow falls from your PiP, how blurry or transparent your shadow is and which direction the shadow falls.

Reflection creates a reflection of your PiP below it in your video frame. Settings control the distance the reflection is from your PiP and how transparent it is.

Flip flips your PiP horizontally or vertically.

3D Settings include a control for adding 3D depth – making your PiP look closer than the videos under it – when used in a 3D project.

Fades add a one-second **Fade In** or **Fade Out** to your PiP. Fading, it should be noted, affects the clip's opacity or transparency level. So a **Fade** will, in effect, make your PiP appear to *dissolve* in or *dissolve* out of your video frame rather than fade in from or out to black. (For more information on adding **Fades**, see page 64.)

PiP Designer Motion presets

Under the **PiP Designer's Motion** tab, you'll find **Path** presets for creating animation movement of your PiP over your other videos.

Applying a **Path** to your PiP is as simple as clicking on a **Path** preset on this panel. (To remove a **Path**, click the **X** in the upper left corner.)

These **Motion Paths** don't change the **Scale** of your PiP – so by default your PiP remains at 100% its size as it follows the **Path**. To **Scale** or even keyframe an animated **Scale** change to your PiP, follow the steps in **Create a Picture-in-Picture in the PiP Designer** on page 150 or **Animate Your Picture-in-Picture in the PiP Designer** on page 151.

When you add a **Path** to your PiP, diamond-shaped keyframes are added to the **Motion Timeline** below the panel's **Preview** window. The **Path** itself will also be visible in the **Preview** window, indicated as a curved line with two or more orange "waypoints."

The diamond-shaped keyframes on the **Timeline** can be moved around to affect the speed of your **Path**. The closer your keyframes are together, the faster your animation will occur.

(For more information on creating and customizing keyframed animations, see **Keyframing** on page 126.)

The "waypoints" on the path in the **Preview Window** are also customizable. Drag them in the panel's **Preview Window** to reshape your **Path**.

Once a Motion Path has been selected, it can be customized by repositioning the Motion keyframes or dragging the Path's "waypoints" to new positions.

Tell stories with multiple video tracks

Although you can create some terrific movies with a single track of video, there are some very powerful and professional storytelling techniques at your disposal when you composite several tracks of audio and video.

Think of multiple tracks of video as a stack, like a stack of photos. In most cases, only the uppermost track in the stack will be visible.

However, if you change the size and position of the images on the uppermost track – or on several tracks – or you make portions of the images on upper tracks transparent, you can display video on several tracks at once and create some very interesting compositions.

You can also add a video clip to an upper track so that your movie cuts away to a separate visual sequence while still playing audio from the track under it.

L-cuts and J-cuts

In addition to the **Picture-in-Picture** techniques discussed earlier in this chapter, multiple tracks of video can be used to create **L-cuts** and **J-cuts**, powerful ways to add visual interest to your movies.

L-cuts and **J-cuts** begin or end with an on-screen storyteller. As he or she speaks, the movie cuts away to related video, supplementing the story he or she is telling with visuals.

Think of a TV news report that features video of a reporter standing in front of a burned-down building, describing the fire that destroyed it.

As he continues speaking, the video cuts away to footage shot earlier of the fire itself. That's an **L-cut**.

A **J-cut**, on the other hand, begins with video of the fire and the reporter's voice describing it – then cuts to video of the reporter finishing his report.

The techniques are similar and the principle is the same: As audio continues from one scene, the video cuts away to another scene.

L-cuts and **J-cuts** are so named because, back in the "primitive" days of film editing, when a segment of film had to be removed and the audio left in place to allow for the placement of alternate video, the cut resembled an "L" – or a "J," depending on whether the beginning or end of the visual portion was replaced with new footage.

As illustrated at the top of page 156, creating an **L-cut** or a **J-cut** is easy with multi-track editing.

1 **Place the main video on the Video 1 track**

This would be the clip of the reporter speaking to the camera or, as in my illustration, the person being interviewed.

L-Cut
Main video starts on top, then goes under "B roll."

J-Cut
"B roll" starts on top, then cuts to reveal main video.

As audio from the main clip continues, video cuts away to or from "B roll" footage.

2   **Place the cutaway video on an upper video track**

Place the cutaway video – the video illustrating what the reporter or the interviewee is talking about– on the **Video 2** track, overlaying the main video (below it, on the PowerDirector **Timeline**).

The cutaway video should be offset from the main video slightly, so that we begin or end – or both – with the main video of the reporter or the interviewee speaking.

Voila! Tweak **Clip B**'s position for maximum effect and you're done! We begin with the reporter or interviewee speaking to the camera and, as he continues to speak, we cut away to footage of what he's describing.

L-cuts and **J-cuts** are very effective for news-style reports as well as for interviews, in which you cut away from the person speaking to separately shot footage of the story he or she is telling.

It's a great way to reinforce with images what's being presented verbally.

By the way, here's some professional vocabulary to impress your friends with. That secondary footage that plays as the main video's audio continues? It's commonly called "**B-roll footage**", a relic from the days when this kind of editing actually did involve pasting in footage from a separate roll of film or video.

Create the "Brady Bunch effect"

Your **Picture-in-Picture** effects need not be limited to a single image. You can resize and position several tracks of video in your video frame to create a split screen or to show several images at once.

Using a number of video tracks and some precise scaling and positioning, you can even create a grid of video images – something we at Muvipix.com call the "Brady Bunch effect."

To create a multi-panel grid, place each grid clip on a separate video track, one above the other.

When a clip is selected on the Timeline or in the Preview window, you'll be able to resize and position it using the corner handles that appear.

1   **Place each video source on a separate track**

Stack up the videos you want to use in your grid by placing each on a separate video track on the **Timeline**, one above the other.

2   **Scale and position each clip**

Select a video clip on your timeline or in the **Preview** window. Use the corner handles and center point that appear when your clip is selected to size and position the clip in the video frame.

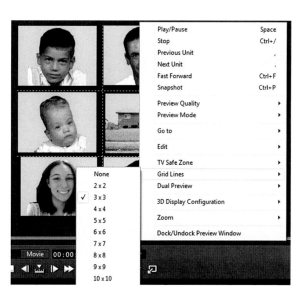

Use Grids as guides

Built into PowerDirector's **Preview** window are a number of grid patterns which you can use to help you in your layouts.

To access these **Grid** overlays, **right-click** on the video in the **Preview** window and select one of the **Grid** options.

This **Preview** window also includes a **TV Safe Zone** guide for ensuring that text and other relevant information isn't cut off when viewed on a TV. We show you how to use it on page 175.

Create PiP Object from an Image.   Create a new shape.   Create a New Hand-Drawn Animation in Paint Designer.   Modify a Selected PiP Object.

The Video Overlay (Pip Objects) Room

PowerDirector comes loaded with dozens of pieces of video "clip art" that can be used in and over your videos. A great many of these clips are animated, and a couple will even display as 3D when used in a stereoscopic 3D project.

To access this library of clips, click the **Video Overlay (PiP Objects) Room** tab along the upper left of the program. A **Search the Library** box in the upper right of the **Room** allows you to do a real-time search for a specific **PiP Object**.

PiP Object clips or **Video Overlays** are tagged to categories, although you can also select **All Content** to see them all at once. When you click on a **PiP Object**, you'll see its animation in your **Preview** window.

New to version 19 are **Sketch Animations**, a collection of scribbly arrows, circles and other shapes that appear to be drawn live over your video. These animations can be customized in a number of ways in the **Sketch Designer**, as discussed in the sidebar on page 164.

In addition to the default set of **PiP Objects** included with PowerDirector, additional **PiP Object** sets can be purchased from CyberLink by clicking the **More Premium Effects** link in the upper left of the panel.

When **PiP Objects** are added to an "upper" video track (**Video 2, Video 3,** etc., which are by default *below* the **Video 1** track on the PowerDirector **Timeline**), they will overlay any video on **Video 1** or other lower video tracks.

You can create and save your own custom-created, animated **PiP Objects** to this room using the **Paint Designer**, as we show you on the facing page. You also have the option of opening any existing **PiP Object** in the **Paint Designer** and modifying it by adding your own animation.

Select a tool, width and size.   Set Duration to control animation speed.

Create an animated Video Overlay with the Paint Designer

The **Paint Designer** is a cool little tool that makes creating animated paint and pencil lines to your videos simple and fun.

Open the **Paint Designer** by going to the **Video Overlay (Pip Objects) Room**, then clicking the pencil icon at the top of the room's panel (as illustrated on page 156).

In the **Paint Designer**, select a drawing **Tool** (pen, crayon, chalk or eraser), set its width and select a color.

Draw across your video frame. Set the **Output Duration/Playback** to set the speed of your animation.

Click the **Save** button and name your animation.

Your animated clip will appear as a **Custom** overlay in the **Video Overlay Room** library.

When added to the timeline above another video, the line you've drawn will appear animated, as if being drawn in real time!

You can also customize existing **PiP Objects** by selecting the object in the **Video Overlay Room** and clicking **Modify Selected Paint Object** at the top of the Room's panel.

Your customized object will also be saved as a new, **Custom Video Overlay**.

Create a PiP Object

As with **Particles**, you can create your own PiP Object from any basic shape or image and even add animation to it. To open this PiP Designer, click the **Create a PiP Object from an Image** along the top of the **Video Overlay Room**.

1 **Select an image**

To create a **PiP Object**, click the **Create a New PiP Object** button along the top of the **Video Overlay (PiP Objects) Room**.

A browse screen will open through which you can select an image file on your hard drive to use as your **PiP Object**. As when you create **Particles** (see page 119), you'll get the best results when your use an irregularly shaped object with transparency through it. PNG files make excellent **PiP Objects**.

You can also use an image with a solid color background. Once this image is added to the **PiP Designer**, you'll have the option of making its background transparent using the **Chroma Key** property. (TIFs, BMPs and PNGs work best. JPEG compression can make for a less than clean key effect.)

2 **Modify the image's properties**

Under the **Properties** tab on the **PiP Designer** you will find a number of modifications that can be applied to your image. You can add a border or outline, a drop shadow or your can rotate or flip the object in 2D or, in a 3D project, in 3D.

At this point, if you are using an image with a solid color background, this background can be made transparent by applying the **Chroma Key** property, as we show you on page 109.

3   **Add animation to your object**

With the object selected, click to select the **Motion** tab. This will give you access to a library of pre-created motion paths.

To apply a path to a selected object on the panel's timeline, click on your selected **Motion** path, as illustrated above.

This path will be added to your object and it will appear as a keyframed property below the object on the **PiP Designer's Timeline**.

Keyframes are tools for creating custom animations, and they appear throughout the program. Keyframes, including those on this panel, be easily created and modified.

You can speed up or slow down any object's motion by dragging the keyframes closer together or further apart. The closer these little diamond-shaped keyframes are on the timeline, the faster your animation will happen.

We discuss keyframing in more detail on page 126.

If you'd like to add a little **Motion Blur** to your object's animation, select the **Motion Blur** option and settings by scrolling down the **Motion** tab.

Click **Save As** or **OK** and name your shape to save your shape to the **Video Overlay (PiP Objects) Room**.

You can re-edit your shape by selecting it in the **Video Overlay (PiP Objects) Room** and clicking on the **Modify Template** button along the top of the room and selecting **Modify PiP Attributes**.

Create and edit PIP Shape overlays

The **Video Overlay (PiP Objects) Room** can launch a workspace for creating and editing shape overlays. This **Shape Designer** includes a library of shapes and preset shape designs as well as preset animations.

Once you save your shape, it will appear under the **Custom** category in the **Video Overlay (Pip Objects) Room.**

To open the **Shape Designer,** click the **Create a New Shape** button along the top of the **Video Overlay (PiP Objects) Room.**

1   **Select a shape**

    Click to select a basic shape from **Shape Types** under the **Properties** tab. Among these shapes are arrows, callouts and thought and speech bubbles.

    Once the shape appears in the **Designer's** preview window, you can resize and position it by dragging on its corner handles.

2   **Customize the shape's look**

    If you'd like, you can select one of the **Shape Preset** looks for your shape. Whether you apply a preset or use the shape as is, you can modify the colors of its border and fill.

    Scroll down through the other **Preferences** and you'll find options for changing the border and for setting the fill and border colors as either solid colors or gradients.

Add text
to shape

3 Add text

If you'd like to add text into your shape, scroll down the **Preferences** and open the **Text** options. Type text into the text box, as illustrated above. Your text will appear on the shape. On this panel you can also modify your text's font, size, alignment and color.

4 Animate your shape

If you'd like to animate your shape's movement, select the **Keyframe** tab on the **Shape Designer**. Position the shape in the preview windows's video frame, toggle on animation and create the shape's custom movement, as we do in the **PiP Designer** on page 154.

Click **Save As** or **OK** and name your **PiP Shape**.

Modify a Sketch Animation

New to version 19 of CyberLink PowerDirector Ultimate's **Video Overlay (PiP Objects) Room** library are **Sketch Animations**, animated overlays that appear as if being hand-drawn in real time onto your video.

Sketch Animations are placed on an upper video track, overlaying a video on a lower track. Once placed, they can be resized and positioned by dragging on the corner handles that appear around the **Sketch** in the **Preview Window** when the **Sketch** clip is selected on the timeline.

Sketch Animations can also be customized in the **Sketch Designer**, opened by double-clicking the **Sketch** clip on your timeline or by selecting the clip on the timeline and clicking the **Designer** Function Button along the top of the **Timeline**.

In the **Sketch Designer**, you can select a custom color for the **Sketch**. You can also change the duration of its animation and its "freeze" time, the length of time the finished sketch remains visible. (In timecode 00;00;00;00, represents hours;minutes;seconds;frames.)

If you like your customized **Sketch** design, click the **Save As** button at the bottom of the **Designer** and name your new **Sketch**. Your saved **Sketch** will appear in the **Custom** category in the **Video Overlay (PiP Objects) Room**.

Set animation duration.   Set image duration.

Title Room Templates

The Title Designer

Editing Motion Graphics Titles

Text Masking Effects

The TV Safe Zone for Titles

Chapter 12

Add Text and Titles

Working with layers of video

With Titles, you can create opening or closing credits for your movie.

You can also use on-screen text to tell or help clarify your movie's story.

Titles and other text can be used to tell your video's story – or to give credit where credit is due.

CyberLink PowerDirector comes loaded with title templates in a variety of categories. Many of these templates include animation, and a number of them come complete with colorful backgrounds.

Existing title templates can be customized. And new titles, complete with 3D-like animation, can be created in the **Title Designer.**

The Title Room

The **Title Room** includes over 100 title templates, many of which include animation, styled text, graphics and backgrounds. The **Ending Credits** template, for instance, is a pre-animated credit roll, which you can customize with your cast and crew's names.

To access this library of title templates, click the **Title Room** tab along the upper left of the program. A **Search the Library** box in the upper right of the **Room** allows you to do a real-time search for a specific title.

Title templates are tagged to categories – although you can also select **All Content** to see them all at once. When you click on a template, you'll see its animation in your **Preview** window.

New to version 19 of CyberLink PowerDirector Ultimate are customizable **Motion Graphics Titles**, which combine cool text and graphic animations. We discuss their uniquely customizable features in the sidebar on page 172.

In addition to the default set of **Titles** included with PowerDirector, additional **Title** sets can be purchased from CyberLink by clicking the **More Premium Effects** link in the upper left of the panel.

Create or modify a Title Template.

When a title is added to an upper video track, your video will show through its transparent areas, appearing as black in the title template.

Add a title from the Title Room

Title templates can be added to the **Video 1** track, or they can be used on an upper video track, overlaying your video.

There are two ways to add a template from the **Title Room** to your timeline.

> **Drag a template from the Title Room** to the **Title** track (illustrated above) or any video track on the **Timeline**.
>
> **Select a template in the Title Room and click the Insert on Selected Track button.** The title will be added to the video track you have selected at the position of the **Timeline** playhead. If you attempt to add a title to a position already occupied by a clip, you will be prompted to select a ripple option, as described in **Add Media Clips to the Timeline** on page 60.

Once you've added a title to your timeline, you can customize its duration and content.

To change a title's duration on your timeline, drag on the title clip's endpoint to extend or shorten it.

If your title includes text animation, extending its length will slow your text animation (a credit roll, for instance). Shortening the title will make the text animation run faster.

Extending or shortening your title clip will not, however, affect the speed of any other animated elements or objects in the template.

To customize the text or the template for a title on your timeline, **double-click** on it – or **right-click** on the title and select **Edit Title**. This will open the **Title Designer.**

Edit selected template in the Title Designer in Basic or Advanced mode.

Create new template in the Title Designer.

The Title Designer

The **Title Designer** is a workspace for creating and customizing your title templates. In this workspace, you can customize a template's text and text style; add, remove and edit graphic elements in the template; and add, remove or edit animation in the template.

The **Title Designer** can be used to customize a title on your timeline or it can be used to edit an existing template in the **Title Room**, in which case your customized title will be permanently added to the **Title Room** for use in a future project.

> To open a title on your timeline in the Title Designer, double-click on the title – or **right-click** on the title and select **Edit Title**.

> To create a custom title based on an existing template, double-click on a template in the **Title Room** or select a template and click the **Modify Selected Template** button at the top of the panel.

> To create a template from scratch, click on the **Create a New Title Template** at the top of the **Title Room** panel, as illustrated above.

The **Title Designer** workspace includes a **Timeline** for creating custom animations, a **Text** panel for customizing your text attributes and a panel with a library of animated **Motion** presets. The **Designer** panel's **Advanced** mode (accessed by clicking the tab above the preview window) includes more options than its default **Basic** mode.

If you've edited a template in the **Title Room**, once you click **Save** or **Save As** in the **Title Designer**, your customized template will be added to the **Custom** category in the **Title Room**.

If you've edited a title clip on your timeline, clicking **Save** will update only the instance of your title template as it appears on your project **Timeline**.

Select the text to customize it and to add or change its properties.

Text animation segment can be shortened or lengthened.

Customize your template's text

To customize the text in a title, select the existing text in the panel's **Preview** window and type over it.

With all or part of the text selected, you can also change its characteristics by using the options on the **Text** panel on the panel's left side. This panel includes a number of styled **Character Presets** as well as options for setting the text's font and size, if it has a font face or border or if it casts a reflection or drop-shadow. If you are using the title in a stereoscopic 3D project, you also have the option of setting its **3D Depth** – how much it seems to float over the background video.

If you are editing the **3D-Like/Default 3D** template, you'll also find options in this panel for rotating your title in 3D space (as illustrated to the right) and for adding 3D textures.

Many titles include animation that is built right into its default text. You really can't edit this animation, other than controlling its speed.

If your animated text on the panel's **Timeline** has a shaded area over its beginning or end (as in the illustration above), this is an indication of an animation that is programmed into part of the title. You can control how fast this animation occurs by widening or shortening this shaded area.

You may also remove this existing text entirely (if you want, for instance, to replace it with your own custom-created animation) by selecting it on the **Title Designer's Timeline** and pressing the **Delete** key on your keyboard.

169

Insert Title   Insert/Remove Particle   Insert Image   Insert/Remove Background

In Advanced mode, new Elements can be added to the panel's timeline, where they can be trimmed, respositioned re-ordered or deleted.

Add more blocks of text to your title

To add or create text in your title template, click the **Insert Title** button at the top of the **Title Designer** panel (as illustrated above) – then click in the **Preview** window and start typing. You can also simply **double-click** in the **Preview** window and start typing.

Once you've added text, it can be styled and colored using the properties listed under the **Text** tab, as we discuss on page 169.

Add Motion to your text

Paths are animation presets that move your text block(s) around your video frame. To add an animated **Path** to a text block in a title template, select the text on the panel's **Timeline** and then select an animation preset from under the **Motion** tab.

When you select a **Path** preset for your selected text, a preview of the effect will appear in the **Preview** window.

To remove any of these animation effects from your text or object, click the big blue **No Effect X** at the top left of the **Motion** panel.

Add an animated Particle to your title

If you click the **Insert Particle** button at the top of the panel (as illustrated above), the program will open into your **Particle Room** (see page 117). The **Particle** you select will be added as an animated element in your title.

This **Particle** effect will appear as a clip on the panel's **Timeline**. By trimming and positioning this **Particle** clip, you can set when, in your title, this effect begins and ends.

Add a custom image or background to your title

The **Insert Image** and **Insert Background** buttons at the top of the panel give you the option of importing custom still photos or graphics into your title.

For information on adding a non-square graphic with no background to your project, see the sidebar on page 122.

Edit elements from your title template

Once added to the panel's **Timeline**, elements can be trimmed and positioned to start or end at a given point.

By dragging on the **Timeline's** track headers, you can rearrange the stacking order of these elements.

To remove text, a background, a graphic or a **Particle** animation from your title template, select that element on the **Title Designer's Timeline** and press the **Delete** key on your keyboard.

Add a Starting or Ending Effect to your title's text

The **Title Designer** includes a number of cool animated effects for your text blocks. These animations can be added as **Starting Effects**, flying or animating your text into the video frame, or **Ending Effects**, flying or animating your text out of the video frame – or both!

Edit Motion Graphics

A number of the templates in the PowerDirector **Titles Room** are tagged as **Motion Graphics**.

These title templates can be edited in the **Title Designer,** where you will find options for customizing the text as well as changing the colors of animated graphics.

As with any customized title, if you select the **Save As** option along the bottom of the **Title Designer,** you can save your new templates to the **Custom** category of **Titles.**

To access this library of animations as well as a tool for adding **Motion Blur** to these animations, select a text block in the **Title Designer** and select the **Effect** tab to the left of the panel.

Under this tab you will find over 75 **Starting Effects** and over 75 **Ending Effects**. To preview the animation of any effect, hover your mouse over the effect's thumbnail. To test drive it with the text in your title, click on the effect's thumbnail.

If your title template already includes animation, its **Effect** will already be selected on this panel. You may replace this animation **Effect** with any other **Starting** or **Ending Effect** – or remove the animation completely.

Once you click on a **Starting** or **Ending Effect**, it is applied to the selected text block in your title. Selecting another effect automatically replaces the previously-selected effect. However, any combination of **Starting Effect** and **Ending Effect** can be added to a block of text – and, of course, different effects can be used on each block of text in your title.

To remove an effect from your text, click on the large **X No Effect** thumbnail.

To apply a **Motion Blur** to your animation, check the option at the bottom of the **Effects** panel. (You may need to scroll a long way down to see it.) The **Motion Blur** effect includes controls for setting the intensity of the blur.

Fade In/Out indicators appear on any element added to the Title Designer timeline.

Fade text or other elements in or out on your title

By default, a one-second **Fade In** and a one-second **Fade Out** are added to any text or other element on your title. These **Fades** are represented as adjustable overlays at either end of the text block or graphic element clip on the **Title Designer's** timeline, as illustrated above.

These **Fade** segments are adjustable. Just drag them longer or shorter right on the timeline. They can also be removed completely by dragging them to the end of the text box or graphic on the timeline.

In fact, the entire clips representing the text or other elements can also be extended, shortened or removed by trimming, dragging or deleting them to meet your custom need.

Text Masking

In addition to the title templates in the **Title Room**, PowerDirector includes a number of **Text Masking** effects.

Text Masking templates are found in the **FX Room** (see page 105), in the **Text Masking** sub-category of **Style Effects**.

Text Blur Masking

Text Sepia Masking

Text X-Ray Masking

Text Shear Masking

173

Customize text

Text Masking cuts your video into the shape of your title and applies a video effect to the video outside this shape – then applies an animation to it.

(You can also create your own custom text masks using the **Mask Designer**, as discussed on page 123.)

As with any effect applied to a clip, **Text Masking** can be customized in the **Effects Settings** panel.

To open the **Effects Settings** panel for a clip, select the clip to which **Text Masking** has been applied and then click the **Effect** Function Button along the top of the **Timeline**.

On the left of the **Effects Settings** panel, you will see the applied **Text Masking** effect as well as any other effects that have been applied to this clip.

Select the **Text Masking** effect from this list, as illustrated.

To customize the text that will be used in this effect, type over the word **CyberLink** under the **Title** property.

Other properties for the effect can be customized by using the sliders – or, for **Motion** animation, you can select an option from the drop-down menu.

When you first attempt to modify any of these properties, a box will pop up warning you that **This operation resets all of the keyframes in this effect. Do you want to continue?** Click **OK**. Otherwise you won't be able to customize your effect at all.

To change your text's font, style or size, click the "**T**" under the **Font** property listing.

The TV Safe Zone

All TVs, including today's modern LCDs and plasma sets, cut a little of the sides, top and bottom off your video. This is an effect called overscan – and some TVs do it more than others.

To ensure that you don't lose any important video information through this effect – especially text – PowerDirector includes an overlay which indicates the **TV Safe Zone** within which you should keep all of your vital video information.

To turn the **Safe Zone** overlay grid on in the main **Preview** window, select a video clip on your **Video 1** track, then **right-click** on the **Preview** window and select the option to turn on the **TV Safe Zone**. (Strangely, this overlay is only visible when a clip on **Video 1** is selected.)

You'll also find a switch for turning on the **TV Safe Zone** in the **Title Designer**, right under that panel's **Preview** window.

We highly recommend you keep your titles and subtitles within this **TV Safe Zone**. Otherwise you risk your title "Gone With the Wind" appearing on some TVs as "one With the Win".

The TV Safe Zone

In addition to the settings you can make in this panel, you can further customize this effect's animation in the **Keyframe Settings** panel, which can be opened by clicking the **Keyframe** button at the bottom of the **Effects Settings** panel.

For more information on creating animations in the **Keyframe Settings** panel, see page 126.

Chapter 13

Add Transitions

Effects for getting from one clip to another

Transitions are fun ways to get from one clip, or one scene, to another.

They can be subtle or showy – fun or barely noticeable.

Transitions add to the tone and feel of your movies.

There are a couple of ways to get from one clip to the next in a movie.

The most basic way is the cut, in which we simply and abruptly move from one clip to another on our timeline. This most simple "transition" serves its purpose: It is, for the most part, invisible. More elaborate transitions draw attention to themselves to varying degrees. Some transitions are subtle and are hardly even noticed. Others are showy and can't help but be noticed.

In any event, a transition is just another storytelling element. It can be used to tell your audience that time has passed between scenes, or that we're moving from one location or point-of-view to another. Good transitions – like a movie's color tone and music – add to your movie's mood and style.

Fade ins and fade outs

Fading into and out of a scene is like raising and lowering a curtain in a stage show. It tells your audience that a major sequence – or maybe the entire show – is beginning or ending.

Fade Ins and **Fade Outs** are added to individual clips on your timeline in PowerDirector.

The simplest way to add a **Fade** to a clip on your timeline is in the **PiP Designer**, which is launched when you **double-click** on a clip on your timeline.

Selecting the option to Enable Fade-In or Enable Fade-Out in the PiP Designer adds a keyframed transition to the Opacity property.

Fade Ins and **Fade Outs** can also be added to your audio and/or video right on the timeline using keyframes, as we show you on page 64.

At the bottom of the **Properties** panel on the **PiP Designer** are the options for **Enabling a Fade-In** or **Enabling a Fade-Out** on your clip.

When you check **Fade** and select one or both of the **Fade** options, diamond-shaped keyframes are added to the **Opacity** property on the **PIP Designer's Timeline**, below its **Preview** window.

By default, these keyframes will create a two-second **Fade-In** animation from 0% to 100% **Opacity** at the beginning of the clip or a **Fade-Out** animation from 100% to 0% **Opacity** at the end of the clip.

By moving the middle keyframe nearer to or farther from the beginning or the end of the clip, you can extend or shorten the length of the **Fade**. (For more information on keyframing in the **PiP Designer**, see **Animate Your Picture-in-Picture** on page 151.)

An important note about **Fade-Ins** and **Fade-Outs** is that they are the results of animations of the **Opacity** property. In other words, when a **Fade In** goes from 0% to 100% **Opacity**, even if it looks like a fade in from black, it is actually an animation from 100% *transparency*.

If your video clip is on the **Video 1** track, then, this animation will appear as a fade in from blackness (since there is nothing on a track below your clip). However, if the video you are applying this animation to is on an upper video track and there is another video on a video track below it, your **Fade-In** will appear more like a *dissolve* from the video on the lower track to this video clip rather than a fade-in from black. We see this happening when a **Fade** is applied to a **Picture-in-Picture,** as we discuss in **PiP Designer Properties** on page 153.

Add a Crossfade

Whenever you add a video clip to your timeline or you shift the position of a clip on your timeline so that it overlaps another clip, a pop-up screen will offer you a number of options (as we discuss on page 60).

If you select the **Crossfade** option, the program will create a dissolve the length of the overlap from one clip to the other.

When you overlap two clips on your timeline and select the option to create a Crossfade, the program will turn the entire overlap into a crossfade transition.

If you click on this overlapped area, you'll see an indicator showing the **Crossfade** transition between the two clips. **Right-click** on this **Crossfade** and select **Modify Transition** to customize its behavior in the **Transition Settings** panel, as we discuss on page 182.

You can also replace a **Crossfade** with another transition by dragging your new selection from the **Transition Room** onto the **Crossfade** on your timeline. This new transition will be the same length as the **Crossfade** was.

The Transition Room

CyberLink PowerDirector, illustrated below, includes a library of over 120 animated transitions.

To access this library of transitions, click the **Transition Room** tab along the upper left of the program. A **Search the Library** box in the upper right of the **Room** allows you to do a real-time search for a specific transition.

The transitions in this room are tagged to categories – although you can also select **All Content** to see them all at once.

When you hover your mouse over a transition, you'll see its animation in your **Preview** window.

A number of these transitions are 3D, which means that, when used in a project set up for stereoscopic 3D, the transition's animated elements will appear to fly right off the screen!

To apply a transition, drag it from the Transition Room to the intersection of two clips.

To replace a transition, simply drag a new one over the existing transition.

Among the library of transitions are two audio transitions, **Constant Gain** and **Constant Power**. Both of these transitions do essentially the same thing – create a smooth audio dissolve from one audio clip to another.

Which you use is up to you. They're very similar, although most experts agree **Constant Gain** makes for a slightly smoother transition.

Apply a transition

To apply a video transition between two clips on your timeline, simply drag it from the **Transition Room** onto the intersection of the clips.

A two-second transition will be added between the clips.

If the clip has both audio and video, a **Constrain Gain** audio transition will also be added automatically to the audio.

Customize a transition

To change the length of an applied transition, **double-click** on it and in the pop-up option panel, change its **Duration Settings**.

When you add your transition directly between two clips, you may notice that the second clip shifts left two seconds so that the clips overlap during the transition. This is called an **Overlap** transition, and it is the type of transition behavior the program applies by default.

Although this behavior sometimes drives users crazy, since it changes the duration of their clips every time they add a transition, this shift is necessary to provide the program the footage it needs to create the transition between the clips.

When you add a transition between two clips, the second clip will jump left to form a 2-second overlap which the program can use to create the transitional segment.

An Overlap transition creates the transitional segment by overlapping the two clips. A Cross transition transitions to black from one clip and then transitions out of black for the other.

This is because throughout any transition between two clips, both clips are on-screen at the same time. When one clip jumps left to overlap the other, this provides the program with the necessary footage from both clips to create this transitional segment.

As an alternative, PowerDirector also includes options for adding transitions without overlapping or shifting your clips' positions.

Drag your transition to one or the other clip rather than exactly between two. This will give one of the clips a transition in from black or a transition out to black – but the transition won't apply to both of your clips.

Add a Cross transition rather than Overlap transition. In a **Cross** transition, the clips remain in position and do not overlap. However, this behavior also creates a very different looking transition.

In a **Cross** transition, the first clip will transition out to a blank screen and then the second clip will transition in (rather than transitioning through the clips).

Options for setting your transition to **Cross** or **Overlap** – as well as for customizing the other elements of your transition – are found in the **Transition Settings** panel, discussed in the next section of this chapter.

To replace one transition with another, simply drag your new selection from the **Transition Room** onto the existing transition on your timeline.

The Transition Settings panel

To launch the **Transition Settings** panel, either select the transition on your timeline and click the **Modify** Function Button, or **right-click** on a transition that you've added to your timeline and click the **Modify** Function Button.

The settings and options available in this panel vary from transition to transition. In fact, some transitions offer only options for setting the transition's **Duration** and selecting whether the transition uses the **Cross** or **Overlap** behavior.

Right-click on a transition and select Modify Transition to open the Transition Settings panel.

In the program's preferences, you can set the default properties for all of your transitions. To access these preferences, click the **Cog** at the top of the program's interface. Transition defaults are set on the **Editing** preferences page.

Add a transition between all the clips in your movie

When you select a transition in the **Transition Room**, three **Apply to All** buttons appear along the top of the **Timeline** – none of which have anything to do with the particular transition you've selected.

Apply Random Transition To All Videos.

Apply Fading Transition to All Videos.

Apply Random Transition to All Audio.

If you click on any of these buttons, you'll be given four options for how it applies its transitions.

Prefix Transition, which adds a random transition or fade in to the beginning of your movie.

Postfix Transition, which adds a random transition or fade out to the end of your movie.

Cross Transition, which adds random transitions or fades so that each clip in your movie transitions from black and then transitions to black.

Overlap Transition, which shifts the positions of all of the clips on your timeline so that they all overlap, applying a random transition or fade from clip to clip.

Remove a transition

To delete a transition you've added between two clips on your timeline, click to select it and press the **Delete** key on your keyboard – or right-click on the transition and select **Remove**.

Create a New Alpha Transition   Modify Selected Alpha Transition

Design or customize a "alpha" transition

The **Transition Designer** is a workspace for customizing and creating **Alpha Transitions**.

Alpha Transitions use the black and white values of an image to create a transitional pattern. The transitional pattern that the **Transition Designer** creates will be based on a dissolve from the blackest black in your image to the whitest white.

In other words, if you provide the **Transition Designer** a gradient image that is black in the center and white around the sides (as illustrated at the top of the facing page), the **Transition Designer** will create from it a transition that begins in the center of the video frame and then widens out.

> To customize an existing transition, select the transition in the **Transition Room** and click the **Modify Selected Alpha Transition** button at the top center of the panel, as illustrated below. (Note that not all of the transitions can be modified.)

> To create a new transition from scratch, click the **Create a New Alpha Transition** at the top center of the **Transition Room**.

Either button launches the **Transition Designer**. However, when you click the **Create a New Alpha Transition** button, you will be prompted to select an image to base your transition on. You can use any color or black & white image to build a transition from – however, using an image that is made up of only black, white and shades of gray makes it easier to determine the animation pattern your transition will use.

At Muvipix.com, we have designed a batch of free black & white patterns you can download and use to create your transitions. Just type "Gradient Wipe Pack" into the product search box.

Your newly created Alpha Transition will create a transitional animation from clip to clip based on the pattern you provide, from the blackest black to the whitest white in your image.

Whether you're modifying an existing transition or creating a custom transition based on your own pattern, the **Transition Designer's Properties** panel (at left) offers you a number of options, including the option to flip the transition's pattern, to add a border between the transitioning clips and to adjust the sharpness of the edge between the transitioning clips.

Shift Progression controls the timing of the transition from one clip to another. By adding a keyframe mid-way through the progression (or dragging at the point of the playhead on the **Progression** timeline, as illustrated below), you can interpolate the transition to vary the speed of the transition's progress.

Once you've created or modified a transition you can load it to the **DirectorZone** or to your personal **CyberLink Cloud** account (see page 226).

With keyframes on the Progression timeline, you can interpolate the transition to animate more quickly or more slowly at the beginning or end.

Creating Subtitles in PowerDirector

Importing Subtitles Into Your Movie

Setting Subtitle Behavior

Chapter 14

Add Subtitles

Optional text for your movie

Subtitles are captions in your movie that are used to clarify a scene's dialog or translate it into another language.

PowerDirector's subtitles can be imprinted on your finished video, or offered as a selectable option for your viewer.

Optional subtitles are another one of those high-level, professional features that come standard with CyberLink PowerDirector Ultimate.

The subtitles you add to your PowerDirector project can be imprinted onto the video itself or they can be added as a selectable option for your viewer.

Your subtitles can be typed right into PowerDirector, or they can be imported into the project from a text file.

Create subtitles in PowerDirector

To access the PowerDirector subtitle creation panel, click the **Subtitle Room** tab in the upper left of the program.

When you add text to your movie in the **Subtitle Room**, you'll need to designate when the subtitle begins in your movie and when it ends. Fortunately, the program makes this process fairly intuitive.

If your **Subtitle Track** isn't visible at the top of the **Timeline** (illustrated at the top of the facing page), enable it by **right-clicking** on the **Timeline's** track headers and checking the **Show Subtitle Track** option.

1   **Locate your subtitle's start point**

    Drag the playhead on your timeline to the point in your movie you'd like your subtitle to begin.

2   **Click the Add Subtitle button**

    The **Add Subtitle** button is the **+** button in the lower left of the **Subtitle Room**.

    A new subtitle listing will be added to this **Room**.

Add a Subtitle Marker.   Double-click to add text.

The text clip is added to the Subtitle Track at the position of the Timeline playhead. Trim and position it in sync with your dialog or video.

3   **Create your subtitle**

Double-click where indicated in the **Subtitle Text** column.

Type your subtitle's text.

Click anywhere else in the **Subtitle Room** to save this subtitle.

For best results, keep it brief. You can add as many subtitles as you'd like to your project.

4   **Set the subtitle's duration**

By default, your subtitle will be 10 seconds long. However, you can trim it to any length by dragging the end of the subtitle inward on your timeline. You can also drag on the subtitle itself to reposition it on your timeline.

If your subtitle is a translation of your movie's dialog, you'll want to synchronize its start and end points to match the dialog.

5   **Select a font**

If you've created several subtitles already, click and drag across the **Subtitle Room** to select all of your existing subtitles.

By default, your subtitles will appear in a basic Windows font. To change the font and font size, click the "**T**" button at the bottom of the **Subtitle Room**.

Select your font, style and font size. These font settings will be applied to all of your selected subtitles. This font will also be applied automatically to any new subtitles you create in your project.

To ensure that none of your subtitles are cut off by TV overscan, it's best to work with **TV Safe Zone** turned on, as we discuss in the sidebar on page 175.

The font you select will be applied to all subtitles you have selected in the Subtitle Room as well as any new subtitles you create.

Create, size and position subtitle markers on the Timeline's Subtitle track, and prepare your subtitle text in a .txt or .srt file.

Import subtitles from a text file

Sometimes, rather than typing your subtitles one at a time into CyberLink PowerDirector, it's easier to work from a script, building all of your movie's subtitles into a text file and then importing that text file into your movie as subtitles.

An important thing to note about importing text is that your imported subtitles will overwrite any existing subtitle text you've added – so it's best to import any subtitles *before* you add any subtitle text manually.

1   **Create your text document**

In your text document, add a line break between each subtitle.

Once you've got your subtitle document completed, save it in a format that PowerDirector can import into the **Subtitle Room**.

Your subtitle document must be saved as either a text (.txt) or SubRip (.srt) file. Virtually any word processor (even Windows Notepad) can save a text document as a .txt file.

2   **Create your subtitle markers**

Set the **Timeline** playhead where you'd like the first subtitle to begin. Click the **Add Subtitle** (**+**) button at the bottom of the Subtitle Room, as illustrated at the top of this page.

Import the .txt or .srt file into your Subtitle Room.

> Move the playhead down the timeline and continue to create
> subtitle markers. You may need to also trim the markers' lengths in
> order to sync your subtitles with the movie's dialog or action.

3   Import your text document

> Click the **Import Subtitles** (file folder) button at the lower-right of
> the **Subtitle Room**.
>
> Browse to and open your text document. The text in your document
> will be automatically loaded into all of the subtitle markers you've
> created.

If you haven't got enough subtitle markers for your document's text, the
program will warn you that not all of your subtitles were used.

If you'd like to manually create additional subtitles, use the steps described
in **Create subtitles in PowerDirector** on page 188.

Set your subtitles' behavior

The subtitles you've
added to your movie can
be imprinted onto the
video you output – in
which case they will
always be visible – or
they can be set up as an
option for your viewer.

Select the type of subtitles you'd like to create.

To set your subtitle's behavior, click the **Select Type of Subtitles** button in the lower right of the **Subtitle Room**, as illustrated on page 188.

>   **Create Subtitles for Discs/Files** creates optional subtitles. Optional subtitles can be toggled on or off on DVDs, BluRays, AVCHD video and MKV video, when played on a compatible player.

>   **Create Subtitles Imprinted on a Video File** permanently prints your subtitles right onto your video.

When you select the **Create Subtitles for Discs/Files,** a sub-menu for turning on and off your subtitles will be automatically added to your disc menu structure.

For more information on disc menu options, see **Chapter 16, Disc Authoring**.

Section 4

Output Your Finished Movie

Produce a Video

Output a Video for a Device

Upload a Video to a Social Media Site

Chapter 15

Output a Video File

Sharing your movie

There are lots of ways to share your finished movie with the world.

You can create a disc; you can post it online – you can even output a file for viewing on a smartphone or other portable device.

PowerDirector includes easy tools for outputting an optimized movie for each of these destinations.

So your movie's finished. Now it's time to share your masterpiece with the world!

PowerDirector gives you a wealth of options for sharing your finished piece – including options for porting your video directly from the program to a number of popular video sharing social media sites.

In fact, there's such a wealth of output options available, it's often hard to decide which is the best for your particular situation.

Produce a video file

PowerDirector offers you the option of outputting your video and/or audio as any of eight file formats.

To access your video output options, click the **Produce** button at the top of the interface.

To access the options for outputting non-3D video or audio, click on the **Standard 2D** tab.

Some profiles for these video formats are only available if your video is 4:3, some are only available if your video is 16:9, some AVC profiles are only available if your video is 9:16. **If your project is set up with the 1:1 square aspect ratio (see page 42) your video can only be output as an MP4: 480x480, 720x720, 1080x1080, 1440x1440 or 2160x2160.**

AVC. A high-quality H.264-compressed format that can output **M2TS, MP4** and **MKV** video files with profiles for outputting 1440x1080 and 1920x1080, 2048x1080 as well as 4K video at 3840x2160 and 4096x2160 at a variety of frame rates. In a 4:3 project, you'll also find profiles for outputting standard definition 720x480 and 720x576 as well as higher definition 2048x1536 and 4096x3072 video. If you are working in a 9:16 (portrait) project, you will find MP4 outputs for 480x720, 720x1280, 1080x1920, 1440x2560 and 2160x3840.

HEVC uses the advanced H.265 codec to produce even higher-quality-per-size files than even AVC (H.264). This option will create **M2TS, MP4** and **MKV** video files with profiles for outputting 1440x1080 and 1920x1080, 2048x1080 as well as 4K video at 3840x2160 and 4096x2160 at a variety of frame rates. In a 4:3 project, you'll also find profiles for outputting standard definition 720x480 and 720x576 as well as higher definition 2048x1536 and 4096x3072 video.

Windows Media produces a **WMV** file, typically used for video viewed online or on a computer. This format includes profiles for 320x180, 640x360, 1280x720, 1920x1080 and 4K video at 3840x2160 and 4096x2160.

XAVC-S is a format for creating ultra-high definition and 4K video as an **MP4**. It includes profiles for outputting video at 1280x720, 1920x1080 and 3840x2160 at a number of frame rates.

AVI, the most common format for outputting editable standard definition video. For both 4:3 and 16:9 video, the DV-AVI profile will output editable video as NTSC 720x480 and PAL 720x576. This format can also be output as uncompressed Windows-AVI in 640x480 or lower resolution.

MPEG-2. A format that includes profiles for outputting DVD-ready 720x480, 720x576, 1280x720, 1440x1080 and BluRay-ready 1920x1080 at both 60i and 24p frame rates.

Image Sequence will output your video's frames as a series of **JPEG** or **PNG** picture files.

Audio output formats (under the musical notes button) include **WMA** (Windows Media Audio), **WAV** and **M4A** audio.

To set where your video will be saved to, click the **Output Folder...** button in the lower right of the **Produce** workspace and browse to a location.

To output your video, click the **Start** button at the bottom of the panel.

3D video outputs

If you're working on a project set up for stereoscopic 3D (see page 78), PowerDirector offers a number of options for sharing your video.

You can output your movie as:

A 3D movie. PowerDirector offers half a dozen formats for outputting your 3D video, in both anaglyphic (red/blue) and stereoscopic MVC (Multi-View Coding). For information on these options, see **Output your 3D video** on page 80.

YouTube 3D. PowerDirector also comes with facilities for loading your 3D video to YouTube. You'll find this option in the **Produce** workspace, under the **Online** tab. To upload your video in 3D, check the option box next to the **Profile** listing.

3D Disc. Finally, you can output your video as a 3D DVD or BluRay disc. To access these options, go to the **Create Disc** workspace and click on the **3D Disc** tab. Otherwise the process for creating your disc and its menus is the same as in **Chapter 16, Disc Authoring**. 3D discs can be output in a number of formats.

The **Anaglyphic** option will output your stereoscopic video channels and shades of red and cyan. Anaglyphic video can be viewed on any device, using inexpensive blue/red glasses.

The **Side-by-Side Half Width L/R** option will output your video with Multi-View Coding (MVC). Although MVC video can also be viewed as 2D on 2D equipment, viewing 3D MVC video requires a 3D monitor or television as well as 3D glasses.

Each video format and profile has an optimum use.

Web video

WMVs were originally designed to be delivery formats for video to be displayed on the internet. Highly compressed and small in size, virtually every streaming video on the Internet was either a Windows Media or a Quicktime file in the Web's early days.

AVC, HEVC and even **MKV** video (all of which can be output as .mp4 files) have more recently become the video formats of choice for video loaded to the Web, due to their smaller file size and higher quality playback.

MP4 video (whether AVC, HEVC or MKV) is the ideal output format for video that you plan to upload to sites like **YouTube, Vimeo** and **Facebook**.

Editable video for use in another project

Editable video is video that you are outputting for use as source media in another project.

The **DV-AVI** profile of AVI is the ideal format for outputting video that will be used in a *standard definition* video project.

For high-definition video, your best choice for outputting video to be used in another *high-definition video* project is the **AVC/M2TS** format with the **AVC 1920x1080 60i** or, if you'd prefer, 60p profile.

Disc-ready video for a third-party DVD or BluRay authoring program.

Video that you're going to use in a DVD or BluRay disc project should be output as MPEG-2s in order to function most efficiently in your disc-authoring program. (In fact, they usually don't require re-encoding to a disc video format.)

DVD-Ready and BluRay-ready **MPEG-2** videos may be burned directly to a disc (to create a menu-less DVD or BluRay) or may be ported to a disc-authoring program (like CyberLink's PowerDVD Ultra).

> **For DVDs,** the ideal MPEG-2 profile is DVD HQ 720x480.

> **For BluRay discs**, the ideal MPEG-2 profile is MPEG-2 1920x1080/60i or 24p (depending on how your disc project is set up).

SVRT Profile Analyzer

The Intelligent SVRT Profile Analyzer

PowerDirector's **Profile Analyzer** will examine the media and effects in your video project and will recommend output formats that produce the highest quality movie with the least re-rendering of your video (commonly known as "smart rendering".)

When you click the **Profile Analyzer** button at the top of the output panel, the program will generate a list of recommendations under an **Intelligent SVRT** (Intelligent Smart Video Rendering Technology) and **Best Matched Formats** tab.

If you'd like to take advantage of this technology, select a recommended format from either the **SVRT** or **Best Matched Format** list and click **OK**. The program will then automatically choose the settings for your output.

Other video output options

Along the bottom of many of the output panels in the **Produce** workspace panel are other options for your video output. Which options are available depends on the format you've chosen.

Fast Video Rendering Technology will optimize the process of rendering your finished video. Some formats allow you to apply **Smart Video Rendering Technology (SVRT)** and some offer you the option of utilizing the **Hardware Video Encoder**.

Dolby Digital 5.1. If your format allows for it, you have the option of creating a video with 5.1 surround sound. This type of audio, however, is most effective if your source video was actually recorded in 5.1 audio.

Some video output templates also include options for **DTS 5.1** (multi-channel technologies from Xperi Corporation, an alternative to Dolby) and **TrueTheater Surround**, CyberLink's proprietary sound enrichment technology.

x.v.Color is a color system that can display a wider range of color than standard RGB. If this option is available for the video format you've selected, **x.v.Color** is nearly always a good choice.

Upload to your CyberLink Cloud. See the sidebar on page 226.

Output your video for a device

PowerDirector can create an optimized video for recording to hard drive camcorders and portable playback devices, including smartphones, Apple products, Sony PSPs and Microsoft Zunes and XBoxes. It can also stream video back to your tape-based miniDV and HDV camcorder for archiving.

To access these output options, click the **Produce** button at the top of the interface, then select the **Device** tab.

The **Android** option creates an optimized video for playing on your smartphone. It includes options for outputting video at 320x180, 640x360, 1280x720 and 1920x1080.

The **Apple** option creates optimized video for iPods, iPhones and iPads at 320x180, 640x360, 1280x720 and 1920x1080 resolutions.

The **Sony** option creates optimized video for Sony PSPs, PS Vitas, PS3s and video Walkmans.

The **Microsoft** option outputs optimized video for Zunes and XBox 360s.

The **DV** option record your video back to your miniDV tape-based camcorder. To use this output, you'll need to have a camcorder that's capable of recording video (most newer camcorders are not) and it must be connected to your computer through a FireWire/IEEE-1394 connection. Cue the tape in your camcorder to the point at which you'd like your recording to begin and then click the **Start** button at the bottom of the panel.

The **HDD** option creates a video file that you can later copy to your hard drive camcorder's storage drive or SD card. The video can be created as either 1440x1080 or 1920x1080 high-def, either NTSC or PAL.

Many output formats include additional options along the bottom of the panel. For more information on these options, see **Other video output options** at the top of page 190.

To set where your video will be saved to, click the **Output Folder...** button in the lower right of the **Produce** workspace and browse to a location.

To output your video, click the **Start** button at the bottom of the panel.

Post your video to a Social Media site

CyberLink PowerDirector includes tools for loading your videos directly to a number of popular video sharing sites under the **Online** tab.

YouTube, Daily Motion, Vimeo and **Youku** include profiles for outputting 320x180, 320x240, 640x360, 640x480, 960x720, 1280x720, 2048x1080 and 2048x1536 video and even 4K at 3840x2160, 4096x2160 and 4096x3072.

Niconico includes profiles for outputting 523x384, 640x360, 800x600, 960x540, 1024x768, 1280x720 and 1920x1080.

Which resolutions are available depend on whether your project is set up for 4:3, 16:9 or 9:16. ("Portrait" 9:16 videos can be uploaded to YouTube or Vimeo.)

Note that the **YouTube** uploader includes the option of uploading 3D video from a 3D project.

Once you've selected a site and a profile, give your video a title, description and, if applicable, add tags and select a video category. You can also select whether your video is viewable to the public or by invitation only.

The first time you use the program to interface with these sites, you will need to authorize it. To authorize the program, just follow the prompts, log in to the site and okay the authorization. After that, you'll be logged in every time.

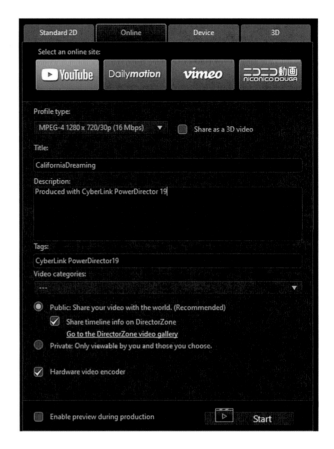

Your output settings may include options for adding a title or tag words to your video, for posting it to a subject category or for setting whether your video is available to the public or to only invited viewers.

To upload your video to a site, click the **Start** button at the bottom of the panel.

Adding Chapters to Your Movie

Adding Content to Your Disc

Selecting a Disc Menu Template

Creating a Custom Menu Template

Saving your Disc Files to Your Hard Drive

2D and 3D Disc Options

Chapter 16

Disc Authoring

Creating DVDs and BluRay discs

Among the most popular ways to share your movies are as DVDs or BluRay discs.

CyberLink PowerDirector includes a whole array of tools for developing menus and creating professional-looking discs.

The process of adding chapters, designing menus and menu systems and burning these completed videos to a DVD or BluRay disc is called **Disc Authoring**.

PowerDirector has a number of easy to use tools for creating great looking discs with lots of cool elements.

Add Chapters to your video

Chapters are points in your movie you'd like your viewer to be able to jump directly to. When you create the menu for your DVD or BluRay disc, links to these **Chapters** will automatically be added to the menu pages as buttons.

In PowerDirector, as you add **Chapters** to your movie, they'll be indicated by markers on the **Chapter Track**, along the top of your **Timeline** (as illustrated on the facing page). If this track isn't visible, **right-click** on the **Timeline's** track headers and ensure that **Show Chapter Track** is checked.

To add **Chapters** to your movie:

1   **Open the Chapter Room**

This room can be opened by selecting the **Chapter Room** tab along the upper left of the program, as illustrated on the facing page.

The **Chapter Room** includes a number of tools for creating and naming your **Chapters**. Three of these options will add your **Chapters** automatically.

Chapters can be added automatically to every clip on your timeline.

Chapters can be added automatically at regular time intervals.

Chapters can be added automatically based on the number of **Chapters** you want in your movie. These **Chapters** will be evenly spread through your movie.

2   **Manually add Chapters**

Chapters can be manually added to and removed from your movie using the buttons along the lower left of the **Chapter Room**.

Timeline Markers

In addition to **Disc Chapter Markers**, you can also add **Timeline Markers** to your timeline. Unlike **Chapter Markers, Timeline Markers** will not link to your disc menus. However, they can be used as reference points for aligning your movie's clips and trims.

To create a **Timeline Marker, right-click** on the ticker along the top of the **Timeline** and select **Add Timeline Marker**. You'll be prompted to name the **Marker** and, when you click **OK**, a little blue **Marker** will be added to the ticker.

Markers can be deleted by **right-clicking** on them and selecting **Remove**.

Auto Chapter options.

Double-click Chapter to rename it.

Remove all Chapters.

Remove Chapter.

Add Chapter at position of the playhead.

Position the **Timeline** playhead at the spot you'd like to place a **Chapter**. (Note that **Chapter 1** is added to your movie automatically.)

Click the **Add Chapter** button at the bottom of the **Chapter Room**. A **Chapter** will automatically be added to the **Chapter Track** and a thumbnail indicating this **Chapter** will appear in the right side of the **Chapter Room**.

The **Chapter** indicators that PowerDirector creates on your timeline are, of course, editable. You can slide them to a new position or, by clicking the button at the bottom of the **Chapter Room**, opt to remove one or all **Chapters** completely.

3D disc authoring

The process of creating menus and scenes for 3D DVDs and BluRay discs is essentially the same as that for authoring 2D discs.

The main difference is that, for full effect, you should select a 3D menu template – and/or you should adjust the 3D Depth (see page 224) for any text so that it appears to float over your menu page.

3   **Name your Chapters**

After you've created one or all of your movie's **Chapters**, you can customize how they'll appear on your DVD or BluRay menu.

Double-click on a **Chapter** listed on the right-side of the **Chapter Room** (as illustrated the previous page) to open the **Rename Chapter** panel. The name you type in this box will be the name that appears as the **Chapter** button on your disc menu.

4   **Customize your Chapter thumbnail**

Each **Chapter** will appear as text and thumbnail button on your disc's **Chapter** menu page(s).

By default, this thumbnail will be the frame of your video directly under the **Chapter** indicator. However, you can also customize it.

To change the thumbnail image for your **Chapter**, ensure that the **Chapter** is selected in the **Chapter Room** and then position the **Timeline** playhead so that the frame you want to use for your thumbnail is displayed in the **Preview** window.

Click the **Set Current Frame as Chapter Thumbnail** button at the bottom of the **Chapter Room**. Note that changing the thumbnail image does not change the location of the **Chapter** marker itself.

To select which image will appear on your menu button to represent a given Chapter, select the Chapter and position the playhead so that the image you want to appear as a thumbnail is visible in the Preview window – then click the Set Current Frame as Chapter Thumbnail button.

Create your disc menus

To select a menu template for your movie, click on the **Create Disc** button at the top of the program's interface to open the disc authoring workspace.

The left side of **Create Disc** workspace has four tabbed panels:

Content. This is where you'll load whatever videos you want to include on your disc. The only limit to the number of videos you can add is how much space each takes up on your disc. An indicator at the bottom of the panel shows you approximately how much space your disc has left.

Menu Preferences. This where you'll select the menu template you'd like your disc to use. In addition to the templates on display in this panel, there are thousands more available for download from the **DirectorZone** – and you have the option of creating one from scratch!

2D Disc and **3D Disc**. This is where you'll set the properties for your disc.

On the right side of this workspace is a big **Preview** window in which you can customize the text and layout of your menus as well as tools for adding background music to a menu page, adding a video clip that shows before the first menu and arranging the order that the menu pages play.

Content

Under the **Content** tab, you can add "bonus" videos to your disc – such as alternative cuts, extra features or a blooper reel. (Illustrated on page 198).

By default, your current video project will appear at the top of the list.

To include additional videos (say bonus features or a blooper reel), click the **Import Additional Videos** button at the top of the panel. (You can also add PowerDirector projects that haven't yet been output by clicking the **Import PowerDirector Projects** button.)

To preview any of these videos, select the video's listing in the **Content** panel and then click the **Play** button.

To rename a video (and simultaneously change how it will be listed on your disc menu), click on the center of the video's listing and overwrite its current name.

To edit a selected video, click the little pencil icon on the right side of the video's listing.

To add Chapters to a video, click the **Set Chapters** button on the right side of the video's listing.

To remove a video, click the trashcan icon on the right side of its listing or simply select it and press the **Delete** key on your keyboard.

Once you've gathered the videos you want to include on your disc, you can drag them into whatever order you'd like.

The first listed video will be the one that is launched when the **Play** button is clicked on your disc's main or **Root Menu**.

The other videos will be available via buttons on a sub-menu, opened by clicking a **Scenes** button on the **Root Menu**.

Select a menu Template

Under the **Menu Preferences** tab, you'll find a library of menu templates.

In addition to the default set of templates included with PowerDirector, if you are logged in to the **DirectorZone**, thousands of additional menu templates can be downloaded free by clicking the **Free Templates** button in the upper left of this panel. For more information on the **DirectorZone**, see the page 222.

You can also modify an existing template or create one from scratch in the **Menu Designer** (as we show you on page 212).

When you click to select a template on this panel, a pop-up panel will display a preview of its **Root Menu** and **Titles/Chapters Menu** designs (including its animation) and will offer you a couple of options:

Apply to All Pages applies this menu template design to all menu pages on your disc.

Apply applies this template only to the menu page currently displayed in the **Preview** window.

Modify (available for some but not all templates) opens the template in the **Menu Designer** (see page 212) so that you can customize its look.

Many of these templates include rather elaborate opening animations, which you can watch by clicking the **Preview** button in the lower right of the interface. To opt not to include this opening animation and set your disc to go directly to your **Root Menu** page, check the **Remove Menu Opening Video** option at the bottom of the panel.

Many menu templates also include default music (which can also be replaced with your own music selection), as on page 210.

If you would prefer to create an "auto launch" disc that has no menus and plays as soon as it's loaded into your disc player, select the **No Menu** template option. A disc with no menus will auto-play as soon as it is loaded into a disc player and will play through all of its videos without menus or prompting.

If you have added optional **Subtitles** to your movie (see **Chapter 14**), the **Root Menu** will automatically include a link to a menu in which your viewer can turn these subtitles on or off.

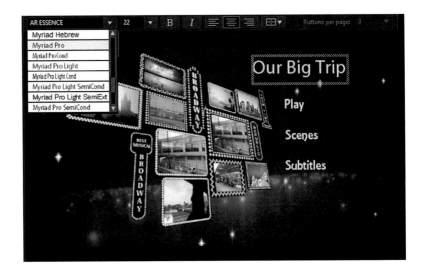

Edit your menu's text

To customize any text on your menu pages – including renaming buttons and links – click to select the text in the **Preview** window.

When a text box is selected in the **Preview** window, an option panel will appear along the top of this window in which you can set your font, size, style and paragraph alignment (as illustrated above).

When applying these text characteristics, you can select and apply them to one or several blocks of text at the same time.

Text blocks and links can also be dragged to any spot on your menu page.

Add menu background music and add a first play video

In the lower right of the **Create Disc** workspace are tools for adding **Background Music** or a **First Play Video** to your disc.

Most menu templates include music, and this music will be added as **Background Music** automatically. But if you'd like to add your own custom music, click the **Set Background Music** button. On the **Select Background Music** panel that opens (illustrated on the facing page), click the **•••** button.

Set First Play Video.   Add music on your computer
                        as your menu background.
Playback Mode Settings.

A **First Play Video** is a short video (an animated logo, for instance) that plays when your disc first loads, before the **Root Menu** appears.

To add a **First Play Video**, click the **Set First Play Video** button and browse to the video file on your computer.

Playback Mode Settings (illustrated below) set the order your videos and menus display on your disc.

On the **Playback Mode Settings** panel, for instance, you can set whether all of the videos linked to a menu page play one after another or if the viewer returns to the menu page after each video plays, as illustrated below.

Playback Mode, by the way, only affects the "bonus" videos you've added to your disc on the **Content** panel. When your viewer selects the option to jump to a **Chapter** in your movie, the video will *always* play through from that point to the end of your movie. It will not return to the menu at the end of that **Chapter**.

To open this option panel, click the **Playback Mode Settings** button in the lower right of the **Create Disc** workspace, as illustrated at the bottom of the facing page.

Select background music from your hard drive.

A First Play Video is a short clip, like an animated logo, that plays as soon as your disc is loaded, before the menu.

Navigate the disc's Menu Structure

At any point, as you're authoring your disc, you have the option of checking out the disc's **Menu Structure**. To open the **Menu Structure** panel, click the button at the top of the **Content** or **Menu Preferences** panel.

The **Menu Structure** panel will display the pathways of your disc, spreading from the **Root Menu** to all of the individual menu pages and videos.

The Root Menu

Your main video

Chapter Menus and video links (pages 1 and 2)

"Bonus" feature videos (pages 1 and 2)

You can get a closer look at the layout of any of your menu pages by selecting it in the **Menu Structure** panel. This menu page will appear in the **Preview** window.

The **Menu Structure** panel is a great workspace for confirming and troubleshooting the arrangement of your disc's pages and links.

To close this panel and return to the **Content** or **Menu Preferences** panel, click the **X** in the upper right corner.

Preview your menus

Before you burn your disc, you'll want to take it for one final test drive.

To do so, click the **Preview** button in the lower right of the **Create Disc** workspace.

You'll be able to navigate using the various buttons and check out the disc's menu structure.

Create and modify templates in the Menu Designer

The **Menu Designer** is a workspace for customizing existing menu templates and creating new menu templates pretty much from scratch.

> **To modify an existing menu template**, select the template on the **Menu Preferences** panel and, on the pop-up option panel, click the **Modify** button. (Note that not all templates can be modified.)

> **To create a menu from scratch**, click the **Create Menu** button at the top left of the **Menu Preferences** panel.

The **Menu Designer** will open to your selected template or to a generic **Root Menu** page with some basic objects and text over a black background.

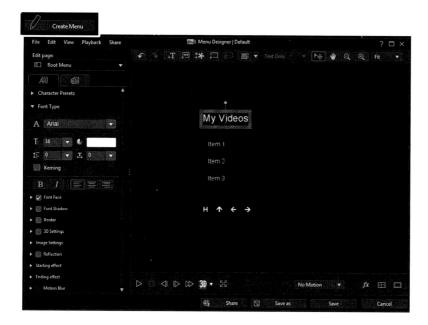

Design a Root Menu, Titles/Chapter Menu and Subtitle Menu

At the top left of the panel is an **Edit Page** drop-down menu. From this menu you can choose whether to edit the **Root Menu** template, the **Titles/Chapter Menu** template or the **Subtitles Menu** template. (All pages in your generated disc menus, other than the **Root Menu** and the **Subtitle Menu,** will be based on the **Titles/Chapter Menu** template.)

Text, objects and button highlights

On the panel to the left of the **Preview** window are two tabs through which you can add, remove and modify elements on your page.

> **Text Properties** define the text characteristics of whatever text block you have selected in the **Preview** window. (You can also drag over or press **Ctrl+a** to select all at once.) On this properties panel you'll find **Character Presets** or text styles, fonts and font properties, **Font Face Settings** (which set the color, transparency and blurriness of the font), options for adding drop shadows under your text, borders around it or reflections under it. If you are working on a menu for a 3D disc, you can also make

your text appear to float over the background by adjusting **3D Depth** under the **3D Settings** (see page 224).

Among these properties are **Starting Effects** and **Ending Effects** from which you can select the animation effect, if any, your text uses to appear on or disappear from your menu page.

Button Properties

Button Properties is a library of custom Navigation Button looks, which you can use to replace a selected button on your menu template. The panel also includes a library of Button Highlights that you can select to appear as highlights when your viewer is navigating over your menu page.

Among the Button Properties are Button Layout templates for arranging the placement of the buttons on your menu page, as illustrated at the bottom of the facing page.

The four graphic buttons, by the way, that appear along the bottom of your menu page template are:

Home, which takes the viewer to the Root Menu page.

Up, which takes the viewer up one menu level.

Left and Right, which the viewer can use to go from page to page if, say, your disc includes several pages of Chapter buttons.

The menu background and additional objects

Along the top and bottom of the Preview window are more tools for adding and replacing elements on your menu page design.

Insert Text allows you to place additional text on the menu page. (After you click the button, click anywhere on the Preview window and start typing.)

Add new text.
Add new button.
Add a graphic.
Add menu background or video before menu.

Import User Video for Menu Opening
Set Background Image or Video

Add motion path to background still.
Add video effect.

No Motion

Add Button creates a new button on your menu page, increasing the number of **Chapters** or links to videos that can appear on any page.

Add Graphic imports additional images or graphics for your menu page's design.

Set Background Image or Video gives you options for adding a video before the menu page or for adding a custom still photo or video as the menu page's background.

In the lower right of the **Preview** window is a drop-down menu for adding motion to your menu background. (This feature is only available if you've added a still photo as your menu background.)

Motion options for **Background Image** include a **Pan, a Zoom, a Zoom and Pan** combination or a **Random** motion.

Background music for your menu is selected in the main **Create Disc** workspace rather than in the **Menu Designer** (see page 210).

When editing the Titles/Chapter Menu pages of your template, you can add, arrange customize the look and resize of your button thumbnails.

Final tweaks

At the lower right of the **Preview** window are additional tools for adding video effects, aligning any objects you have selected and a switch for toggling on the **TV Safe Zone** (see page 175).

Click the **Play** button below the **Preview** window to test drive the menu page (including a video before the menu, if you've selected that option.)

Save your DVDs and BluRay disc files to your hard drive

PowerDirector offers you the option of burning your disc directly from the program, creating a **Folder** of your DVD or BluRay disc files or creating an **ISO** file.

An **ISO** is an image file, a format in which all of the video, audio and menu navigation is saved as a single file. Appropriately, this file will have .iso as its suffix.

ISO files and disc **folders** can be saved or archived to your computer's hard drive and then burned to a DVD or BluRay disc whenever you need to output a fresh copy.

To save your DVD or BluRay disc as an image file or as a set of folders, click on the **Burn in 2D** or **Burn in 3D button** in the lower right of the **Create Disc** workspace. On the option screen that opens, select the **Save as Disc Image** and/or **Create a Folder** option and set the save to location.

For information on burning an **ISO** or **folder** as a DVD or BluRay disc, see page 218.

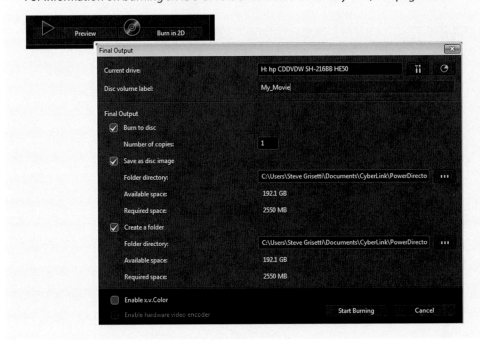

Save your template design

A complete menu template consists of a design for the **Root Menu**, a design for the **Titles/Chapter Menu** and a design for the **Subtitles Menu** (though they'll likely share a similar style or theme).

When you've finished these three page menu designs, click the **Save** button at the bottom of the panel and name your template. Your template will be saved to the **Custom Menu Preference**s library.

 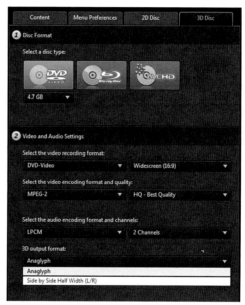

The 2D Disc and 3D Disc option panels

Under the **2D Disc** and **3D Disc** tabs are options for setting the type of disc you want to output and your audio and video preferences

- A **DVD** is a standard definition video, the most common disc produced. DVDs can be burned to a 4.7 gigabyte disc, an 8.5 gigabyte dual-layer disc or, on rare occasions, a 1.4 gigabyte discs. Audio and video options for a DVD include the option for setting whether the disc is a 4:3 or 16:9 video and if the audio is 2-channel stereo or 5.1 surround sound.

- A **BluRay Disc** is a high-definition video. BluRays can be burned to 25 gigabyte or 50 gigabyte discs and, on rare occasions, a 100 and a 128 gigabyte disc. A BluRay's video can be encoded as either H.264 (AVC) or MPEG-2. BluRay audio can be either 2-channel stereo or 5.1 surround sound.

- An **AVCHD** disc is, essentially, a BluRay video burned to a DVD disc. This disc can only be played on a BluRay player (and not on all of them) and its audio can be either 2 channel stereo or 5.1 audio. AVCHD video can also be saved to a removable disc, memory card or memory stick and then played back on a computer.

As a rule of thumb, a standard **DVD can hold about 70-80 minutes of video** at full quality. A dual-layer DVD can hold about twice that.

A 25 gigabyte **BluRay disc can hold about two hours of high-definition video**. A 50 gigabyte disc can hold about twice that.

A 4.7 gigabyte **DVD disc can old about 20 minutes of AVCHD video**, and an 8.5 gigabyte dual-layer DVD disc can hold about twice that.

Options for your 3D Disc properties are similar to those for 2D Discs, except that 3D Discs include an option for setting the disc's **3D Output Format**.

> The **Anaglyphic** option will output your stereoscopic video channels as shades of red and cyan. Anaglyphic video can be viewed on any device, using inexpensive blue/red glasses.

> The **Side-by-Side Half Width L/R** option will output your video with Multi-View Coding (MVC). MVC video requires a 3D monitor or TV to view in 3D (although this video will play as 2D on a standard TV also). This 3D format also does not support standard 2D disc menus or optional subtitles.

> The **3D-BD** option is only available for BluRay discs and can only be played on a BD 3D player and viewed on a 3D television.

Burn a folder or ISO file to a disc

Most disc authoring tools (including Nero and CyberLink's PowerDVD) include options for saving your finished DVD or BluRay disc files as a **VIDEO_TS folder** or an **ISO** file. (See the sidebar on page 206.)

CyberLink offers for purchase a great little disc utility called Power2Go, which can burn your DVD or BluRay folder or ISO file as a playable DVD or BluRay disc. However, you can also burn discs from these files using the indispensable *free* program **ImgBurn** (a free download from www.imgburn.com).

Select the option to Write Files/Folders to Disc from main ImgBurn page.

Select a folder as your source and then browse to and select your DVD's VIDEO_TS folder. Click Burn.

To burn a DVD, AVCHD or BluRay disc from a folder using ImgBurn, select **Write Files/Folders to Disc** from the ImgBurn main menu (as illustrated on the facing page). When the software opens, click the **Source/Folder** button and browse to and select the **VIDEO_TS** folder that was created when you burned your DVD or AVCHD files to a folder, then click the **Burn** button.

To burn a DVD, AVCHD or BluRay disc from an ISO file using ImgBurn, select **Write Image File to Disc** from the ImgBurn main menu. When the software opens, click the **Source** button and browse to and select the **ISO** file, then click the **Burn** button.

ImgBurn will automatically unpack the ISO file and create a playable DVD or BluRay, with menus, from its files.

Select the option to Write Files/Folders to Disc from main ImgBurn page.

Browse to select your ISO file as your Source, then click Burn.

The one downside to ImgBurn is that it comes with some extra bloatware, most of which you'd probably prefer not to have on your computer. (In fact, some anti-virus software flags ImgBurn as malware. Which it's not.)

If you just watch the installation screens for the program and opt out of its add-ons, you'll be fine. In fact, you'll be rewarded with one of the best free programs on the internet.

For a free tutorial and how to safely install and use ImgBurn, just go to Muvipix.com, type "ImgBurn" in our product search box and click the magnifying glass.

Chapter 17

An Appendix
More things worth knowing

In addition to the basic workings of the program, there are a number of additional things about the program worth knowing.

Here, in no particular order, is some extra knowledge for making your PowerDirector editing experience a little bit easier.

What's the difference between PowerDirector Ultra, Ultimate, the CyberLink Bundle and PowerDirector 365?

The main difference between the Ultra, Ultimate and Bundle versions of the program and the 365 versions is that the former are one-time purchases. Pay once and the program is yours for life. While the 365 versions are subscription plans. Once you end your subscription, you'll no longer have access to the program.

Which is the better value depends on how often you plan to upgrade. If you plan to upgrade whenever a new version of the program comes out, the 365 subscription plans can ultimately save you a few dollars. However, if you like paying once and owning the program forever, the standard lifetime licenses are a better buy.

For a complete comparison of the various versions of the programs and the tools and templates bundled with each, go to cyberlink.com/products/powerdirector-video-editing-software and click the **Comparison** button.

What is the DirectorZone?

The **DirectorZone** is a free online library of effects and templates, available to any PowerDirector user. To access this library, simply click on the blue **Free Templates** button you'll find throughout the program. You can also access this library by logging on to the web site at directorzone.cyberlink.com.

To sign up or log in to the **DirectorZone**, open the program's preferences (by clicking on the **cog** at the top center of the interface) and select the **DirectorZone** page.

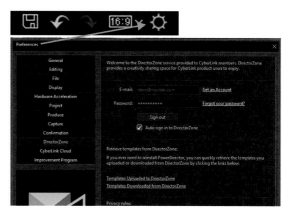

Among the cool stuff available at the **DZ** are **PiP Objects**, **Particle** effects, **Title** templates, **Disc Menu** templates, **Magic Movie Styles**, **Sound Clips** and sound effects and **Video Presets** for creating stylish video looks.

As of the writing of this book, there are over half a million templates and effects available.

Most of the effects and templates available at the **DirectorZone** were created by fellow users.

And, in fact, you can upload your own designs simply by clicking the **Share** button along the bottom of any **Designer** panel or by clicking the **Globe** icon at the top left of many of the **Rooms**, as discussed in **What is the CyberLink Cloud?** on page 226.

How can I grab a frame or take a snapshot of my video?

To save a still photo "snapshot" of the video currently visible in the **Preview** window, click the **Take Snapshot** (camera) button along the bottom of the Preview window.

A **Snapshot** can be saved from a 2D project as a .bmp, .jpg, .gif or .png. A **Snapshot** can be saved from a 3D project as an .mpo or .jps.

Once you save a **Snapshot** of your video, this still will be added to your **Media Room** library and you can then use it in your video project.

To select the type of image file your **Snapshot** will be saved as and where this file will be saved to, open the program's preferences (by clicking the **cog** at the top center of the interface) and go to the **File** page.

If you'd like to just freeze the playback of your video rather than grab a frame and save it as a still photo, you can simply **right-click** on a clip on your timeline and select **Edit Video/Image**, then **Freeze Frame**. A 5-second still of the current video frame will be inserted into your project's timeline.

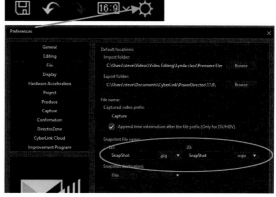

The program also includes a very sophisticated tool for freezing your videos as well as for adding cool time shift effects to your playback. For information on using this new **Freeze Frame** tool, see **The Video Speed Designer** on page 72.

What are "shadow files?"

Shadow Files are proxy files that PowerDirector automatically creates in order to make the editing of high-resolution video more efficient.

While you are editing a high-definition video format that stresses your system resources, PowerDirector automatically creates low resolution versions of your video file, which it uses in place of the larger, more challenging files throughout the editing process.

When you are ready to produce your finished video or disc, PowerDirector then applies your editing data to your original, full-definition video files in order to produce a full quality output.

To enable or disable **Shadow File** editing, open the program's preferences (click on the **Cog** at the top center of the interface) and go to the **General** page.

Where can I set my project to 5.1 surround sound rather than stereo?

You can access this option by opening the program's preferences (by clicking on the **Cog** at the top center of the interface) and going to the **Audio Channel** preference on the **General** page.

When you output your finished video, select the 5.1 option, as discussed on page 200 and page 217.

What is 3D Depth?

3D Depth is a setting for text or titles that are used in a stereoscopic 3D project.

In a 3D project, adjusting the **3D Depth** can make your text or a picture-in-picture appear closer in 3D space, as if your text or video clip is floating over the rest of your video.

What is Intelligent SVRT?

Intelligent SVRT stands for Intelligent Smart Video Rendering Technology, tech that the program uses to analyze your source video and recommend the fastest and most efficient output format for your project.

To view **Intelligent SRVT** information while you are editing, toggle on the **SVRT Track** on your timeline (**right-click** on the track headers and ensure that **Show SVRT Track** is checked).

The green line along the **SRVT Track** displays the segments of your video that will not need to be re-rendered if you use a SRVT-recommended output format.

To re-open this panel while you are editing, **double-click** on the green or red bar along the **SVRT Track**.

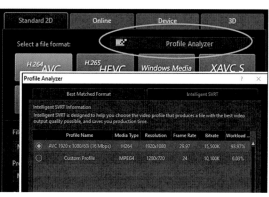

An **SRVT** analysis and recommendation can also be run in the **Produce** workspace by clicking on the **Profile Analyzer** button at the top of the **Standard 2D** or **3D** panel. In the **Intelligent SRVT** pop-up panel, the program will recommend the most efficient output settings for your project's video.

To accept the **SRVT's** recommendation, click the panel's **OK** button. The program will automatically set your output specs to this setting.

How can I add a time stamp to my videos?

The **Time Stamp** effect can be found in the **FX Room**, in the **Style Effect** category and the **Text Masking** sub-category.

To display the **Time Stamp** over your movie, drag this effect to the **FX Track** and then stretch it to cover your entire movie.

To customize how and where the **Time Stamp** appears, select the **Time Stamp** effect and click the **Modify** Function Button along the top of the **Timeline**.

In the **Effects Settings** panel that opens, you'll be able to set the font, color and where in your video frame the **Time Stamp** appears.

What are Favorites?

Favorites, as you'd expect, are video effects or transitions that you especially like and you'd like easy access to.

To add an effect or transition to your **Favorites**, **right-click** on it in the **FX Room** or **Transition Room** and select **Add To/My Favorites**. The effect or transition can then be easily accessed by clicking that Room's **My Favorites** tag.

You'll also find the option to "favorite" **Character Presets** in the **Menu Designer** and the **Title Designer**. To save a **Character Preset** as a **Favorite**, select the preset you'd like to **Favorite** and then click the **Save Currently Selected Character as Preset** button to the right of the **Character Presets/Character Types** drop-down menu.

What is the CyberLink Cloud?

The **CyberLink Cloud** is an online storage bank (included free with most versions of PowerDirector) in which you can save videos, effects and templates that you've created, and then access them from any computer anywhere in the world, as long as it's logged into your **Cloud** account. This includes devices like phones and tablets, that are running the mobile version of PowerDirector.

Among the media you can save to the **CyberLink Cloud** are:

  Program preferences and
     customized output profiles.

  Produced videos or video segments.

  PiP Objects, Particles, Transitions, Paint Animations, Title Effects and **Disc Menu Templates** that you've customized or created.

Unlike designs that you upload to the **DirectorZone**, templates and other media that you back up to the **Cloud** will only be available to a computer or mobile device that is logged into *your* personal **Cloud** account. In other words, the **Cloud** is your personal backup and storage area.

To back up or restore your program preferences, open the **Preferences** by clicking the **Cog** at the top center of the program and go to the **Cloud** page. Click the **Back up** or **Restore** button.

Upload a new template or effect to the Cloud.

Download from the Cloud.

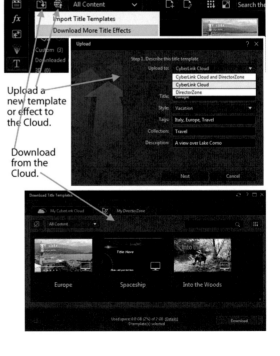

To upload effects or templates that you've created to your **Cloud** account (or to the **DirectorZone**), click the **Globe** icon in the upper left of the **Room** into which you've saved your custom effect or template, as illustrated to the right. (You can also click the **Share** button from many **Designer** workspaces.)

On the **Upload** panel, illustrated at the bottom of the facing page, you'll find options for naming and categorizing your design as well as for indicating whether your design will upload to your personal **Cloud**, be shared with your fellow videomakers on the **DirectorZone** site or both.

To access effects, media and templates you've uploaded to your **Cloud** account, click on the **Folder** icon in the upper left of an effect or template **Room** and select **Download More**, as illustrated on the bottom of the facing page.

How do I blur a face like on TV's COPS?

Occasionally you run into a scene that requires a little censorship.

Sometimes it's to hide something offensive in your movie. Sometimes there's someone in your movie who doesn't want to be in your movie.

The simplest way to salvage the footage is to blur the area of the video you want to censor beyond recognition – the way they blur or pixelate faces of people and license plate numbers on the TV show COPS.

This effect can be created using traditional keyframing, as described on the following pages, or by using the **Motion Tracker**. For information on tracking an object or person in your video and then hiding this object or the person's face with a **Mosaic Effect**, see the discussion of the **Motion Tracker**, starting on page 112.

1 **Place your clip on Video 1**

Ensure that the video clip you want to censor is on the **Video 1** track.

Move the playhead to the beginning of the clip, or to the point at which you'd like your blur to begin.

2 **Add the Mosaic effect to the FX Track**

Open the video effects library by clicking on the **FX Room** tab in the upper left of the program.

Locate the **Mosaic** effect, in the **Style Effect** category, and drag it to the **FX Track** on the **Timeline**, along the **Video 1** clip you want to censor.

Stretch or trim the length of this effect so that it begins where you'd like your blur to begin and ends where you'd like it to end.

The entire video segment covered by the **Mosaic** effect will then be pixelated beyond recognition.

3 **Open the Mosaic Effects Settings**

Select **Mosaic** effect on the **FX Track** and then click the **Effect** Function Button along the top of the **Timeline**.

The **Effects Settings** panel will open. If you'd like, you can fine tune the **Mosaic** effect. A **Height** and **Width** of about 10 seems to work best for me.

Adjust the Mosaic settings to blur your video.

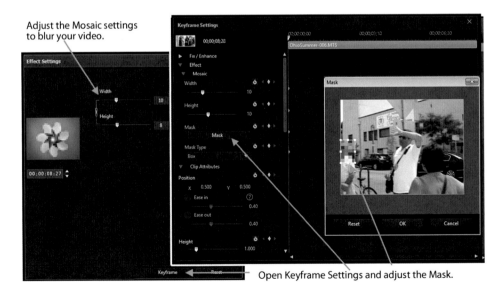

Open Keyframe Settings and adjust the Mask.

3   Open Keyframe Settings

Click the **Keyframe** button on the **Effects Settings** panel. The **Keyframes Settings** panel will open, displaying settings for the **Mosaic** effect.

4   Create an initial Mosaic Mask motion keyframe

Position the playhead at the beginning of your clip and click the **Add Keyframe** button next to the **Mask** button. A diamond-shaped keyframe will be added to the keyframe workspace at the position of the playhead.

5   Place a Mosaic Mask

Click the **Mask** button, as illustrated at the bottom of the facing page.

6   Size and position the Effects Mask

When the **Mask** panel opens, drag the corner handles to size and position the **Effects Mask** so that only object or person you're trying to censor is blurred.

Click **OK**.

7   **Create a closing Mosaic Mask motion keyframe**

Assuming the person or object you're trying to censor moves around the video frame over the course of the clip, you'll need to animate the **Mask's** position to follow him or it.

Drag the **Keyframe Settings** playhead or press the **End** button on your keyboard so that the playhead is moved to the end of the effect's **Timeline**.

Move the playhead to the end of the effect's timeline and reposition the Mask as needed. A new keyframe will be automatically created.

Click the **Mask** button again and reposition the blurred area on the **Mask** panel so that it is again over the person or object you want to censor.

Click **OK**.

A new keyframe will be created on the **Mask's** timeline.

8   **Create additional keyframes**

Slowly drag the playhead from the beginning to the end of the **Keyframe's Settings Timeline**, watching the **Preview** window as you do.

Whenever the person or object you're trying to censor slips out from behind the **Mosaic** blur, click the **Mask** button and reposition the blur. When you click **OK**, a new keyframe will be created for that **Effects Mask** position.

When you've finished, the program will create an animation for your **Mosaic** area so that this pixelation follows the person or object you want to censor throughout your clip.

Need some Basic Training?

To get you up and running, we've created a free 8-part Basic Training tutorial series for CyberLink PowerDirector.

You'll find it along the left side of this page: Muvipix.com/cpd19.php – or go to YouTube and search "Muvipix PowerDirector 19 Basic Training".

Hope you'll become a part of our friendly Muvipix community!

Index

Index

Made in the USA
Monee, IL
30 August 2021